Modelling EXCITING Writing

Sara Miller McCune founded SAGE Publishing in 1965 to support the dissemination of usable knowledge and educate a global community. SAGE publishes more than 1000 journals and over 800 new books each year, spanning a wide range of subject areas. Our growing selection of library products includes archives, data, case studies and video. SAGE remains majority owned by our founder and after her lifetime will become owned by a charitable trust that secures the company's continued independence.

Los Angeles | London | New Delhi | Singapore | Washington DC | Melbourne

Modelling EXCITING Writing

A GUIDE FOR PRIMARY TEACHING

ADAM BUSHNELL
ROB SMITH
DAVID WAUGH

Los Angeles | London | New Delhi
Singapore | Washington DC | Melbourne

Learning Matters
An imprint of SAGE Publications Ltd
1 Oliver's Yard
55 City Road
London EC1Y 1SP

SAGE Publications Inc.
2455 Teller Road
Thousand Oaks, California 91320

SAGE Publications India Pvt Ltd
B 1/I 1 Mohan Cooperative Industrial Area
Mathura Road
New Delhi 110 044

SAGE Publications Asia-Pacific Pte Ltd
3 Church Street
#10-04 Samsung Hub
Singapore 049483

Editor: Amy Thornton
Senior Project Editor: Chris Marke
Project Management: Deer Park Productions
Marketing Manager: Lorna Patkai
Cover design: Wendy Scott
Typeset by: C&M Digitals (P) Ltd, Chennai, India
Printed in the UK

First published in 2019 by Learning Matters Ltd

© Adam Bushnell, Rob Smith and David Waugh 2019

Library of Congress Control Number 2018953019

British Library Cataloguing in Publication Data

A catalogue record for this book is available from the British Library

ISBN 978-1-5264-4932-0
ISBN 978-1-5264-4933-7 (pbk)

At SAGE we take sustainability seriously. Most of our products are printed in the UK using responsibly sourced papers and boards. When we print overseas we ensure sustainable papers are used as measured by the PREPS grading system. We undertake an annual audit to monitor our sustainability.

CONTENTS

ACKNOWLEDGEMENTS

We are grateful to Tom Maxwell for producing a case study of his work with Finley Paterson of Sherburn Primary School, Durham, and to Finley and his parents for allowing us to publish his writing. We would also like to thank Laura Middlemass, Christine Hodgson and Year 4 at Lumley Junior School for the case study on wildlife; we are grateful to Laura for writing the case study for us. We greatly appreciate Shaun Marshall's case study and reflection, which gave an insight into a school's writing process.

Our thanks go to all the teachers and pupils whose good practice and exciting writing have inspired our own writing and provided case studies to exemplify our own ideas. In particular, we are grateful to Frankie O'Reilly for contributing a chapter on using technology to engage reluctant readers and aid writing, which we feel enhances our book and adds an interesting dimension.

We'd also like to thank Kath, who was always there with the right words.

ABOUT THE AUTHORS

Adam Bushnell is a full-time author who delivers creative writing workshops in the UK and internationally in both state and private education to all ages.

His books have been selected by the School Library Association for the *Boys into Books* recommended reading list. Previously a teacher, Adam now also delivers CPD to teachers and others working in education on how to inspire writing in the classroom.

Rob Smith is the creator and curator of the award-winning website The Literacy Shed, www. literacyshed.com. After a 12-year career as a primary teacher, Rob now delivers writing workshops to students and professional development for teachers across the UK and around the world. Rob was a contributing author for *Beyond Early Writing* and is now writing his own English ideas website as well as creating a range of apps for teachers.

David Waugh lectures in Primary English at Durham University. He has published extensively on primary English. David is a former deputy head teacher, was Head of the Education Department at the University of Hull and was Regional Adviser for ITT for the National Strategies from 2008–10. He has written and co-written or edited more than 40 books on primary education. As well as his educational writing, David also writes children's stories and regularly teaches in schools. In 2017 he wrote *The Wishroom* with 45 children from 15 East Durham schools.

About the additional contributor

Frankie O'Reilly is a full-time primary teacher with a first class degree in media. For a number of years, Frankie has been subject leader for English and a Lead Teacher for 'Literature Works' – a programme to promote the innovative teaching of reading. Frankie's passion for bridging literature and technology led her to develop an augmented reality children's book, *The Boy with his Head Stuck in a Book* (Tyne Bridge Publishing, 2017) which has been celebrated in numerous reviews including *The Times Educational Supplement*. Frankie's Young Adult novel was long listed for a Novel Opening and Synopsis award and her short story 'The Woman in the Water' was published by Severance Publications in 2017.

INTRODUCTION

We wrote this book for both new and experienced primary school teachers. As teachers ourselves, we know the expectation to help our children to produce high-quality and varied examples of writing. We know that the writing process can be difficult for some children, a percentage of whom are disaffected writers. But we also know that by modelling writing, we are showing children how to make the writing process achievable. We have written this book in order to showcase our passion and experience in modelling a whole range of writing techniques. We hope that the kind of modelled writing in this book will engage teachers and make children motivated in their own writing.

All of the authors in this book are teachers and now spend their time modelling writing for children while being observed by other teachers in order to show writing processes. We now do this in our role as visiting authors or as deliverers of professional development in primary schools. The case studies gathered in this book have been collected on lesson observations of teachers. These have been the most effective modelled writing lessons that we have seen regarding modelling writing, and we wanted to share them here in order to give practical, real-life lessons that genuinely work. We are passionate about sharing good practice in schools and we hope that you find ideas, lessons and resources that can be used immediately in the classroom in order to develop your own skills in modelling writing.

Unlike some other academic books and teaching resources, we wanted this book to be a blend of theory and practice, with as many ideas as possible that can be used in lessons on an everyday basis. By including modern teaching techniques such as using film and augmented reality, blended with relatively rarely taught writing themes such as fanfiction and writing with and for children, we have tried to bring something to the classroom that will develop teachers' confidence and ability in modelling writing.

In Chapter 1, we have begun with Spelling, Punctuation and Grammar (SPaG) ideas, as this can sometimes be an area which teachers find dull to teach. We have tried to show some new and exciting ways to make SPaG more enjoyable to learn about and also more enjoyable for us to teach.

Chapter 2 examines the importance of reading to develop our own writing skills and those of the children we teach. The chapter is full of ideas of books and samples of texts which showcase a wide range of writing techniques which we can emulate in the classroom when modelling writing.

In Chapter 3, we look at how to scaffold writing for children and examine how this aids both confidence and ability. But the chapter goes on to suggest how to reduce the amount of support we offer to help the children become independent writers.

When modelling writing we are writing for children as our audience. Chapter 4 shows how writing for children can impact on their writing, and also how it develops our own skills in the writing process and our own methods of teaching writing.

Writing with children is something that we have found very powerful in developing both professionally and personally. In Chapter 5, we look at a project that resulted in a published book produced by children from 15 different primary schools.

In Chapter 6, we examine how we can model descriptive writing, focusing on narrative stories, character and settings. The chapter looks at a range of descriptive techniques including the use of dialogue to reveal character, props to enhance setting descriptions and common structures used in short stories.

In Chapter 7, poetry writing is examined in a variety of forms, including hip hop, kennings, rhyming couplets, saga poetry, figurative language and performance poetry. There are lots of examples of each within the chapter that can be replicated or developed further in the classroom.

Fanfiction has gained in popularity in recent years. Chapter 8 provides practical examples of how this can be used in the classroom to model writing in the same style as J.K. Rowling, Cressida Cowell or others. Popular franchises such as Star Wars, Rainbow Fairies and Adventure Time are all used as opportunities to develop children's writing.

In Chapter 9, film is examined, and we consider how it can be used as a model as an alternative to a written text. There are recommended animations that can be used to model writing in the classroom that lead to effective independent writing.

In Chapter 10, the retelling of fiction and non-fiction is looked at in a variety of ways, including school trips, jokes, storytelling and using five sensory descriptions. But the chapter also examines how memory and point of view affected this and how both we and children retell events that we have personally experienced.

Engaging reluctant readers and writers by using technology is the subject for Chapter 11. In this chapter, Frankie O'Reilly looks at the use of apps and augmented reality and how this can impact on the motivation that children have to write.

Each of these chapters follows the same structure, and features Teachers' Standards at the beginning, before moving on to key questions which will be explored throughout. The case studies demonstrate how the theory is put into practice in the classroom. But there are also sections with a research focus to show the academic theory behind each recommendation. There are practical examples and guidance as to how this can be applied to your own daily teaching methods in modelling writing.

We hope that you enjoy reading our ideas and that you will gain a greater understanding and motivation to model writing: writing that both you and the children will find *exciting*.

Adam Bushnell
Rob Smith
David Waugh
November 2018

WRITING AND SPELLING, PUNCTUATION AND GRAMMAR

KEY QUESTIONS

*   How can spelling, punctuation and grammar be an integral part of creative writing?
*   Can SPaG motivate and inspire children to write?
*   How can we embed SPaG development in effective writing development?
*   How can we maintain high-quality writing when teaching children about SPaG?

Introduction

Children are assessed on spelling, punctuation and grammar throughout their primary years. The SATs for Year 6 featured heavily on the news in recent years, with parents, teachers and pupils all voicing their opinions about the assessments. Some teachers agreed with the tests and their level of difficulty, others did not.

Professor Richard Hudson, who was the main advisor on creating the SATs papers, explained why he supported the SPaG tests by stating:

> *I am convinced that children should understand something about how their language works (KAL – knowledge about language), and should be able to talk about simple grammatical patterns both in English and in foreign languages; so, they should learn something about phonology, spelling patterns, vocabulary and grammar.*

Hudson, 2015

However, authors and children's laureates Michael Rosen and Michael Morpurgo disagree with the tests completely. Rosen criticised the prescriptive nature of 'right answers' in tests when language is something he describes as 'ever changing and academics cannot agree on whether there is a subjunctive in English' (2015). Morpurgo (2017) agrees and adds, 'when it comes to creativity, I think SATs sit like a dark spider all over creativity in the classroom' (2017).

Indeed, the authors of the SPaG section of the National Curriculum have expressed serious doubts about both the curriculum and the tests. The section below comprises extracts from a *Guardian Education* article (Mansell, 2017)

Guardian: 9 May 2017

> *Now Richard Hudson, the academic who says he bears most responsibility for introducing the fronted adverbial, has said the process through which the national curriculum was changed under Michael Gove, the former education secretary, was 'chaotic'. He admits it was not based on good research evidence and says he feels many teachers are not equipped to teach it.*

> *Hudson's comments mean that all four of an expert panel that advised the government on placing greater emphasis on traditional grammar in its primary curriculum now have serious reservations about either the tests, or the curriculum development process.*

> *… But he does admit there was 'chaos' in the process of developing what is a controversial curriculum. 'To give you an idea of how chaotic things were, when [the curriculum panel] was originally put together, we had about four meetings and were supposed to be devising a grammar curriculum to cover the whole of compulsory education: primary and secondary.*

> *'We started off with the primary curriculum, which we were a bit unconfident about as none of us had much experience of primary education [Myhill had, in fact, done some research into grammar in primary schools], and were looking forward to getting stuck into the real thing: secondary.*

> *'Then the DfE pulled the plug by saying: "We are not going to do any secondary curriculum." So what was published [the primary curriculum] was meant to be about building the foundations for the real thing. But that's all there is.'*

In this chapter we argue that, whatever one's opinion on the tests themselves, an understanding of spelling, punctuation and grammar is essential for children and adults. It is part of every subject taught in the primary classroom. We will show how meaningful and engaging activities can be used to help children to learn about their language in context. While there may be questions about the content of the curriculum and the tests associated with it, we maintain that it is helpful to share a common vocabulary about language with pupils and we emphasise that this is generally best acquired through reading and writing rather than in discrete grammar lessons. Interestingly, Deborah Myhill, whose work is cited in the research focus below, was one of the four authors of the SPaG curriculum.

FOCUS ON RESEARCH

Myhill, Lines and Watson (2011) examined ways of developing children's writing and discovered that actively engaging children with grammar through writing was more effective than teaching grammar as a separate topic. They found that children were less likely to see the purpose of grammatical knowledge when it was taught out of the context of actual writing; they asserted that children can become more aware to the *infinite possibilities* of the English language through studying how language works, and that this can enable them to evaluate others' language use. They suggest that:

a writing curriculum which draws attention to the grammar of writing in an embedded and purposeful way at relevant points in the learning is a more positive way forward. In this way, young writers are introduced to what we have called 'a repertoire of infinite possibilities', explicitly showing them how different ways of shaping sentences or texts, and ... different choices of words can generate different possibilities for meaning-making.

Myhill et al., 2012:3

Frequently, when we read something that is grammatically incorrect, such as 'the red, big bus', we know that something is wrong. We know that it should read 'the big, red bus', but often we cannot explain why it is grammatically incorrect. We just know. This is because if we read often we become more aware of grammatical structures, and spotting grammatical errors becomes instinctive. Children can recognise errors in texts when they are fluent readers, exposed frequently to the correct spelling, punctuation and grammar.

The reason that the 'red, big bus' in incorrect is because adjectives must follow a particular order. According to the *Cambridge Dictionary* (2018), if there are multiple adjectives before a noun then the order is: opinion, size, physical quality, shape, age, colour, origin, material, type and purpose. This means that size goes before colour, so 'the red, big bus' becomes 'the big, red bus'. This also means that we would never have 'green, ancient, huge dragons'. But we could have 'huge, ancient, green dragons'.

Knowing grammatical rules is important and ways of teaching and learning these rules in creative ways will be explored throughout this chapter. But by encouraging children to read, we reinforce instinctive knowledge of grammar and also spelling and punctuation. The more children read, the more they are exposed to SPaG and the easier it is to teach and learn about it.

Modelling writing and developing knowledge about language

Look at the dialogue below and consider how the Year 4 teacher is engaging children in the writing process while developing their knowledge about language.

Teacher (indicating two sentences on the board)	Right, there's my story opening (reads): Sarah was lying in bed. She heard a loud noise. It seemed to be coming from just outside her bedroom window. Is everybody happy with that? Would you want to read the rest of the story if you read that at the beginning of a book? Could I improve it at all?
Jack	Well, I think it ought to be more dramatic, like it could start with the noise and Sarah waking up.
Lucy	Yeah, you could have a word like *crash* or *thud* first.
Adam	Yeah, you know, one of those words that sounds like the noise.
Teacher	Great idea. We could use an onomatopoeic word. Can anyone suggest one? (He writes on the board as children suggest *crunch, crackle, splat, bong, crash* and *thwack*.)
Teacher	OK, we've got some ideas for words to start the story; can you improve my writing a bit more?
Lily	Well, you could make it just one sentence like: *Crash: Sarah was woken by a loud sound from just outside her bedroom window.*
Teacher	Excellent. I like the way you've added an adjective like *loud*.
Faith	You could add an adverb like *suddenly* to show how she was woken.
Teacher	Brilliant ideas. Right, before I finalise my story opening I need everyone's help. Can you work in pairs and write your own version of the story opening? Make sure you include at least one adverb and adjective so that we get a picture of what was happening.

The teacher has developed a dialogue with the class and has subjected his deliberately rather dull writing to their critical scrutiny. He has welcomed their ideas and has used some linguistic terminology in context. This has been reinforced as he has invited the children's ideas. There is a gradual shift of responsibility from the teacher modelling writing to the children giving ideas and then writing independently. The next stage could be for the children to read some of their story openings and for the teacher to edit and revise his, reading and re-reading as he does so and perhaps thinking aloud to model the writing process. For example, *I think it might sound better if I shifted the adverbial to the beginning of the sentence* or *What if I put in something about how Sarah felt when she was woken by the noise? Can anyone suggest any adjectives which might describe that?*

Vygotsky asserted: 'What the child can do in cooperation today, he can do alone tomorrow' (Vygotsky, 1986: 188). The teacher in the example above is enabling children to see the writing process in action and to contribute to it, while developing their potential to work independently. Vygotsky referred to this as the *zone of proximal development*: the distance between the actual development level as determined by independent problem solving and the level of potential development as determined through problem solving under adult guidance or in collaboration with more capable peers (Vygotsky 1978: 86).

This approach might be termed *interactive writing* (Roth and Guinee, 2011) and involves teacher and pupils working together 'to construct a meaningful text while discussing the details of the writing process' (ibid.: 333). Crucially, Roth and Guinee argue that 'The instruction does not follow a specified sequence but evolves from the teacher's understanding of the students' strengths and needs' (ibid.: 335). This approach therefore makes demands upon the teacher, who needs to be confident about her or his subject knowledge and prepared occasionally to admit to ignorance. This can bring children into a collective approach to learning when, for instance, the teacher is unsure about a spelling and asks people to look it up in a dictionary or discuss what spellings might be possible.

Key features of this type of modelling include:

- *considering audience:* keeping the intended readership at the forefront of one's thinking and the children's, so that an appropriate style and language use is discussed and referred to regularly;
- *articulating the process of writing:* showing that real writers draft, edit and revise and make mistakes and have strategies for correcting them;
- *demonstrating the application of spelling and grammar rules:* this can include making use of appropriate terminology and making deliberate mistakes, for example in spelling, punctuation and subject–verb agreement;
- *re-reading regularly:* checking that writing is accurate, language and sentence structure is varied, and vocabulary interesting, varied and accessible.

In the case studies which follow, note how teachers make use of some of these strategies to develop children's writing and their knowledge about language.

FOCUS ON RESEARCH

Higgins (2015) conducted a meta-analysis of research on teaching literacy and drew some interesting conclusions about the teaching of writing:

- evidence (Graham et al., 2012) indicates it is important to expose pupils to a *variety of forms of writing* and to practise these so that they learn to write for a variety of purposes and master different genres of writing (e.g. description, narration, persuasion or argumentation, information and explanatory texts);
- seeing examples of good writing in these different forms and being given positive feedback when they develop key features is essential;
- teach explicit strategies. For example, in descriptive writing one approach which has been shown to be effective is to link written descriptions with the senses: *What did you see? How did it look? What sounds did you hear? What did you touch? How did it feel? What could you smell? What did you taste?*

Formal and informal writing

Teaching children to write in a variety of styles can be challenging. Children need to consider what it is that they are writing, who it is for, what the purpose of the writing is and whether it is formal or informal, depending on the audience. This is known as GAPS: *genre, audience, purpose* and *style.*

The more children are exposed to a variety of texts, the more they begin to identify these changes in style. For example, when they talk to their friends, children use informal language, but when they are expected to write a non-chronological report using topic-related language this must be formal language. Making this shift can be challenging for children.

In order to recognise the difference between formal and informal language, we can use familiar texts to assist. In the case study below, the teacher has been sharing *The Gruffalo* with her Reception class. The rhythm and the repetition of the book had helped the class to memorise the text almost completely. She could point to the words and the class could recite the text on every page. It is written in formal language and, as it is such a familiar text to the children in the case study, it could be used to compare the difference between formal and informal language.

CASE STUDY

RECEPTION CLASS ORALLY RETELLING *THE GRUFFALO* IN AN INFORMAL STYLE

Nicola, a Reception teacher in the North East of England, had finished reading *The Gruffalo* by Julia Donaldson to her class. They had read it several times previously and the class joined in with the reading. She then showed the class another copy of the book but explained that it had been written differently. This was *The Gruffalo in Scots* retold by James Robertson. It begins:

> *A moose took a dauner through the deep, mirk widd. A tod saw the moose and the moose looked guid.*

> *Whaur are ye aff tae, wee broon moose? Will ye no hae yer denner in ma deep-doon hoose?*

> *That's awfie kind o ye, Tod, but I'll no –I'm gonnae hae ma denner wi a gruffalo.*

The children laughed and said that the words were wrong. Nicola explained that it had been written in the way that some people from Scotland spoke. She went on to say that we all speak differently depending on where we come from. The class were told that this was called dialect and accent.

She then asked the class the different ways in which they have heard people say 'hello'. The answers ranged from 'hiya' to 'ey up' to 'all right' to 'hi'. Nicola went on to model rewriting *The Gruffalo* in North East dialect. The children gave her suggestions and she acted as scribe. She wrote:

A mouse ganned down the dene. A fox saw the mouse and he looked all right.

Where you ganning, little, brown mouse? Do you want some bait back at mine?

That's dead nice an tha, fox, but no – I'm gonna have me bait with a Gruffalo.

The children thought it was very funny to write in this way. Nicola asked them why it was so funny and they told her that books don't sound like that. She then asked the children to retell an eight-part, pictorial storyboard of *The Gruffalo* in talk partners, but to do it in the same way that she had modelled. The children then took the storyboards and orally retold the story using informal, local dialect. Nicola then gave the children photocopied sheets with characters from *The Gruffalo*. They had empty speech bubbles for the children to insert the words the characters said.

The more able wrote in sentences, the middle ability wrote words and phrases, and the lower-ability children used their phonics knowledge to create sound blends with support.

The case study illustrates how children can be helped to understand differences in regional dialect. It also helped the children to understand that when we talk to our friends we use a different form of language from when we write. It was a lesson that formed the beginning of a comprehension of the difference between formal and informal writing. *The Gruffalo in Scots* is one of many Scottish dialect books. Others include: *The Gruffalo's Wean, There was a Wee Lassie Who Swallowed a Midgie* and *Geordie's Mingin' Medicine*.

When children grasp the concept of the difference between formal and informal writing, even in the early years, it helps them to check for grammatical errors in their own writing. They begin to realise that sentences such as 'He was dead frightened' or 'She learned the class lots about butterflies' are not grammatically correct. By looking at the ways in which we adapt our language for our audience when speaking, we can help children to see the way we change from formal to informal language. Once this has been understood, this adaptation of language can be seen in our writing too.

ACTIVITY 1   CORRECTING SPAG

Show a KS1 or lower KS2 class the animation 'Usain Bolt – The Boy Who Could Fly' from Youtube or the Literacy Shed.
   https://www.youtube.com/watch?v=qtujkNnCYCc
   https://www.literacyshed.com/usain.html

(Continued)

(Continued)

In the beginning, Usain's mother says, 'You're gonna be late!' Usain then runs off chanting to himself, 'Not gonna be late. Not gonna be late. Not gonna be late.'

- Could the children change this informal speech into formal language?
- What other sentences or phrases could the children change?
- What other texts or animations contain informal language? How could these be used to teach the difference between formal and informal writing?

Tell the children that changing writing from one form to another is like magic. Tell them that they are going to practise this magic. They will become witches and wizards, but instead of using wands, they are going to use pens. Give them phrases and sentences such as 'I wuv you', 'I dunno' or 'Whatcha gonna learn us?' and ask them to change them to grammatically correct phrases and sentences.

The children are seeing the magic of language. They are seeing that making a small change can make a big difference to words. In this example, they are transforming sentences from the incorrect to the correct: from the informal to the formal.

- What other incorrect grammar do you hear regularly in the classroom?
- How can you use this activity or similar ones to correct this grammar?
- What displays in the classroom might help to fix grammatical errors? Could you incorporate the witch, wizard or magical theme to this display?

FOCUS ON RESEARCH

Wyse and Torgerson (2017: 1043) examined studies on effective teaching and learning of grammar and concluded:

> supporting primary/elementary pupils' grammar is most likely to require teachers intervening during the writing process, and interacting to discuss the use of grammar in relation to the overall purpose of the writing task and the purpose of the writing. The necessity to use technical terms, such as subordinate clause or subjunctive with pupils, remains a question open to research, but it is doubtful that attention to such terms is beneficial. It is probable that adopting everyday language to discuss improvements in the use of grammar in writing will be more beneficial. Small-group and whole-class teaching that includes a focus on the actual use of grammar in real examples of writing (including professionally produced pieces, realistic examples produced by teachers including 'think aloud' live drafting of text and drafts of pupils' writing) may also be more effective.

Chain writing

Chain writing is an activity which can help pupils to develop their sentence writing skills. The sentences are very structured and the activity is teacher-led, but it can lead to independent and complex sentence writing. For example, ask the children to write the word 'the' followed by two adjectives to describe a dragon, mermaid or fairy; then add the correct noun, followed by the word 'was'; then add a verb, an adverb and finally a preposition followed by 'the' and another noun. This gives children the experience to create their own sentences in a structured way and increases confidence to go on to create independent writing. They might create sentences such as:

The huge, scary dragon was flying rapidly in the sky.

The beautiful, swift mermaid was swimming majestically in the ocean.

The magical, tiny fairy was floating happily in the forest.

Once children are confident with this method of chain writing, they can independently add extra adjectives and adverbs and figurative language devices such as similes or alliteration throughout the sentence. So, 'The huge, scary dragon was flying rapidly in the sky' might become 'The huge, scary dragon was flying like a rocket rapidly in the cold, blue sky'.

As well as being part of formal lessons, chain writing can also be an engaging and informal activity. It can be a perfect ten-minute morning task, before registration is taken or as an activity to complete as a warm up to a literacy lesson. The children work with partners, taking turns to add words or phrases. They might use a strip of paper each to write on and fold, swapping their papers on each turn. The person who goes first starts by adding a boy's name to the top of a strip of paper, then they add the word 'met' and swap papers with their partner. They then write a girl's name and swap. A preposition is then added, remembering that each time a new word or phrase is written the paper is folded over. The pair swap again and write 'he wore' and add some clothing and do the same for 'she wore'. After swapping, they write 'he said' and write speech between inverted commas. Another swap and the children write 'she said' then more speech between inverted commas. There is then one final swap and the children write 'they then' and finish with a last event.

They can then unfold their papers and read others' nonsense narratives.

An example could be: *Zac Efron met Katy Perry at the bus station. He wore pink leggings. She wore a baseball cap backwards. He said, 'I like cheese.' She said, 'My unicorn has run away.' They then had a party.*

Making writing fun, but still teaching the skills to enhance knowledge of SPaG, is important for every classroom. An example of this can be seen in the case study below.

CASE STUDY

YEAR 1 CLASS DEVELOPING DESCRIPTIVE WRITING

Liam was teaching his Year 1 class how to add more detail to their descriptions. The class had been describing landscapes and focusing on adjectives. Liam showed images on an

(Continued)

(Continued)

interactive whiteboard. He then wrote a word bank of adjectives that the children suggested for each new setting. There was a tropical beach scene, a dark cave, an icy landscape, a dense forest, a coral reef.

The class had been previously studying nouns and verbs. He reviewed these grammatical terms and modelled short sentences that included nouns, verbs and now adjectives, using the settings as stimulus. He wrote short sentences such as 'The hot beach had swaying trees.' and 'The spooky cave had dripping rocks.' The children then identified the nouns, verbs and adjectives in each sentence.

The class then collected whiteboards and pens and returned to the carpet. Liam asked them to write 'The' on their board using a capital letter to show that this was the beginning of their sentence. They were then asked to imagine their own setting or one of the places displayed on the board. They were asked to add an adjective. The less able used phonics cards to help them sound out their words. The children then added the word 'had' and were asked to think of verbs and nouns to finish their sentences like the ones he had modelled. Liam offered several suggestions and wrote these on the board.

After adding a full stop, the children shared their sentences with each other.

The class then went to their desks. Liam supported the less able, while the class wrote their whiteboard sentences into their books. If they completed these, the children were to independently write more sentences for their chosen setting or for new ones. The sentences were shared, first with talk partners and then volunteers read to the class as a plenary.

The case study shows that by giving the children structure in their sentences they can use these taught skills to move towards more independent writing. As children develop confidence in using nouns, verbs and adjectives correctly in their writing, they can begin to add other word types such as adverbs, prepositions and conjunctions. The terms for each word type become fully understood through practice and repetition.

ACTIVITY 2

As teachers, our constant challenge is to help children move away from heavily modelled, scaffolded writing to independent, confident writing. The basic sentence-making, as in the case study above, is a good first step, but the next step is to move towards richer descriptive language.

Show the children some colour paint charts that are available from DIY stores, Pinterest or online. Ask them to match different flowers to different themed colour charts.

For example, which shade of blue does the bluebell best match? Is it royal blue, ocean blue, midnight blue or one of the others? Which shade of yellow does the daffodil best match? Is it sunbeam yellow, corn yellow, golden yellow or one of the others? Which shade of red does the poppy best match? Is it cherry red, crimson red, candy red or one of the others?

This kind of colour description really enhances basic sentences into much richer language. 'The hot beach had swaying trees' becomes 'The hot beach with lemon zest sand had swaying, spinach green trees.'

- What can be used instead of flowers?
- How can adverbs extend this type of sentence?
- What else can be used to enhance description other than colour?

FOCUS ON RESEARCH

GRAMMATICAL TERMINOLOGY

Horton and Bingle (2014: 17) argue that terminology should be introduced when children are exploring and using language:

> You would not teach children to swim without introducing terms such as breast stroke, front crawl and sculling in order to communicate precise meaning and it is more than likely that you would do this whilst swimming. It is no different from teaching children about language: terms such as adverbial, subordinate clause and collective noun can all be used effectively whilst engaged in a writing activity. The use of a metalanguage will give children the tools with which to discuss choices and manipulate language confidently and powerfully.

Conclusion

In this chapter we have considered how spelling, punctuation and grammar can be taught and learned effectively and have examined strategies which enable teachers to develop children's subject knowledge in conjunction with their writing. We have cited research which suggests that this is the most effective way for children to understand the terminology and concepts associated with SPaG, while seeing them in context. We would argue that this approach is more likely to lead to long-term knowledge and understanding, especially as it enables children to use grammatical terminology in real writing situations, often involving teacher modelling.

A typical reaction to grammatical terminology from trainee teachers who did not learn it in their schooldays is to maintain that they have managed to succeed educationally, and write well, without ever using terms like fronted adverbial or subordinate clause, so why is it necessary for them to learn these terms now and then teach them to children? Of course, the pragmatic answer is that, as teachers, they will be judged by the success of their pupils in tests and, currently, SPaG is tested annually.

A better answer might be to draw a parallel between learning grammar and learning a skill such as driving. Most people seem to regard themselves as good drivers, but how many could lift the bonnet of their car and identify various parts of the engine? A little knowledge and some terminology is certainly helpful when it comes to checking oil using a *dipstick,* topping up the *screenwash container,* and attaching *high tension leads* to *battery terminals* when the car won't start. Without some basic terminology, motorists have to pay mechanics to perform simple tasks which they could easily do themselves after looking at a simple manual.

Think back to your driving lessons. The instructor used terms like *gearstick, clutch, brake, accelerator* and *indicator* rather than describing the items by the actions they performed (better a *steering wheel* than 'the round thing in front of you that you turn when you want to change direction'). A basic knowledge of grammatical terminology provides us with the vocabulary to understand why something is incorrect and to explain this to others. It enables us to discuss our reading and writing using a common vocabulary, and it also prepares us for learning other languages. How much more useful and precise it is to understand and use a term like *adjective* rather than referring to 'describing words which describe things'!

Further reading

For guidance on teaching grammar, spelling and punctuation, see the following:

Horton, S. and Bingle, B. (2014) *Lessons in Teaching Grammar in Primary Schools.* London: Sage.
Waugh, D., Warner, C. and Waugh, R. (2016) *Teaching Grammar, Punctuation and Spelling in Primary Schools* (2nd edition). London: Sage (3rd edition to be published in 2019).

Recommended websites

Usain Bolt animation – https://www.youtube.com/watch?v=qtujkNnCYCc and https://www.literacy shed.com/usain.html
Colour chart images – https://www.pinterest.co.uk search Colour charts.

References

Cambridge Dictionary – Order of Adjectives Cambridge Dictionary online https://dictionary. cambridge.org/grammar/british-grammar/about-adjectives-and-adverbs/adjectives-order (accessed 30 January 2018).
Donaldson, J., Scheffler, A. and Robertson, J. (2012) *The Gruffalo in Scots.* Edinburgh: Itchy Coo.

Graham, S., Bollinger, A., Booth Olson, C., D'Aoust, C., MacArthur, C., McCutchen, D. and Olinghouse, N. (2012) *Teaching Elementary School Students to be Effective Writers: A Practice Guide* (NCEE 2012-4058). Washington, DC: National Center for Education Evaluation and Regional Assistance, Institute of Education Sciences, US Department of Education.

Higgins, S. (2015) Research-based approaches to teaching writing, in Waugh, D., Bushnell, A. and Neaum, S. (eds), *Beyond Early Writing*. Northwich: Critical.

Horton, S. and Bingle, B. (2014) *Lessons in Teaching Grammar in Primary Schools*. London: Sage.

Hudson, R. (2015) *The SPaG Tests and Grammar in the National Curriculum* Available from http://dickhudson.com/spag-tests/

Mansell, W. (2017) Battle on the adverbials front: grammar advisers raise worries about Sats tests and teaching. *Guardian*. 9 May. https://www.theguardian.com/education/2017/may/09/fronted-adverbials-sats-grammar-test-primary (accessed on 27 June 2018).

Morpurgo, M. (2017) 'Dark spider' of Sats is bringing fear to classrooms. *Times Educational Supplement*. https://www.tes.com/news/morpurgo-dark-spider-sats-bringing-fear-classrooms (accessed on 27 June 2018).

Myhill, D.A., Jones, S.M., Lines, H. and Watson, A. (2012) Re-thinking grammar: the impact of embedded grammar teaching on students' writing and students' metalinguistic understanding. *Research Papers in Education* 27(2): 139–66.

Myhill, D., Lines, H. and Watson, A. (2011) *Making Meaning with Grammar: A Repertoire of Possibilities*. Exeter: University of Exeter.

Rosen, M. (2015) *Dear Ms Morgan: In Grammar There Isn't Always One Right Answer*. Available from https://www.theguardian.com/education/2015/nov/03/morgan-grammar-test-right-answer-spag-english-spelling-punctuation-grammar

Roth, K. and Guinee, K. (2011) Ten minutes a day: the impact of interactive writing instruction on first graders' independent writing. *Journal of Early Childhood Literacy* 11(3): 331–61.

Wyse, D. and Torgerson, C. (2017) Experimental trials and 'what works?' in education: the case of grammar for writing. *British Educational Research Journal* 43(6): 1019–47.

Vygotsky, L.S. (1986) *Thought and Language* (trans., rev. and ed. A. Kozulin). Cambridge, MA: MIT Press.

Vygotsky, L.S. (1978) *Mind in Society: The Development of Higher Psychological Processes*. Cambridge, MA: Harvard University Press.

2
READING FOR WRITING

KEY QUESTIONS

- Why is reading important to develop writing?
- What is the best way to use reading as a model for writing?
- Which texts are best used to develop creative writing?
- How do we inspire children to want to read?

Introduction

Most teachers would agree that children who read for pleasure frequently will be better writers; however, as discussed in the chapter 'Film as a model text', there are many pupils who do not read for pleasure often and, even when they do read for pleasure, they don't read *high-quality* novels. It is important that we teach these children to glean writing techniques from high-quality authors. It seems that perhaps those pupils who read a lot do this without consciously thinking about it, but for many children this needs to be a deliberate process.

In order to effectively *read like a writer*, it is important that children are exposed to a wide range of high-quality texts. Teacher knowledge here is vital in order for the children to make links between texts with similar themes, structures or sentence constructions. However, Cremin et al. (2009) suggest that some practitioners 'may not be sufficiently familiar with a diverse enough range of writers to enable them to foster reader development, make book recommendations to individuals and promote independent reading for pleasure' (ibid.: 4).

If this is the case, then these *practitioners* need to deepen their own knowledge of high-quality texts. It will take time for teachers to build this knowledge if they are reading whole texts. One resource from which to acquire a wide range of text extracts for comparison is www.lovereading4kids.co.uk.

Hopefully, by using extracts of texts, teachers are able to develop their knowledge of the text quickly. They can then use whole texts to slowly build up their own library to use when teaching reading and writing. The Lovereading4kids.co.uk website is a library of extracts which is searchable via age group and/or theme.

Extracts are not only ideal as a medium through which teachers can familiarise themselves with text, they are also perfect for use with the children. Six weeks per term, six terms per year often gives teachers the challenge of racing to complete a full novel with their class. Sometimes the reading session can become a sprint to finish with little discussion around the language, techniques or organisation of the novel. Enjoyment is lost as children can struggle to digest the narrative and its construction. Prose (2012) suggests that 'Slowing down and analysing as little as three to four pages of text will enable children to absorb the features with the aid of the teacher–pupil discussion' (ibid.: 26). This is not to say that completing a novel is no longer necessary. If it is the case, and only extracts are read in each English lesson, then additional reading opportunities could be provided so that children have the opportunity to complete the text and experience the enjoyment and sense of achievement that this brings.

FOCUS ON RESEARCH

In Canada, the Ontario report of the expert panel on early reading, *Early Reading Strategy* (Ontario, 2003), states:

> *Reading aloud to children helps them to develop a love of good literature, motivation to pursue reading on their own, and familiarity with a variety of genres, including*

(Continued)

(Continued)

non-fiction. It provides them with new vocabulary, exposes them to a variety of lit-erature, and contributes to their oral and written language development. Reading aloud should occur every day in the early stage of reading instruction to stimulate the children's interest in books and reading.

Ibid.: 24.

In England the National Curriculum (DfE, 2013) now emphasises the importance of reading to children throughout their primary education.

CASE STUDY

YEAR 6 CLASS USING THE BOOK *WILD BOY* AS A STIMULUS FOR WRITING

Khalid, a Year 6 teacher, did not begin his lesson by sharing the learning intention, but rather told the class that they were going to analyse a section of text that they had read the previous day. The class had read the prologue of *Wild Boy* by Rob Lloyd Jones, pages 7–14, together as their class read. Through the tension and excitement in the prologue, the children were left ready to engage with the text and to read Chapter 1 in this lesson.

First, Khalid asked the children to describe what had happened in the prologue the previous day; the children enthusiastically volunteered a range of answers describing different sections of the plot. Khalid then asked the children how the story started; one of the children described the opening of the story with words such as *gloomy* and *foggy*. At this point, Khalid asked the children to collect the words which the author used to describe the fog and the way that the fog moved. Collectively, they found a variety of examples: *crept, crawled, slithered, curled, smothered, swallowing, rose* and *rolling in*.

The extract that the children needed to read to demonstrate this technique was:

Above the houses the sky turned from black to dingy brown as a thick fog crept over the city. The monstrous mud-brown cloud rose from the river. It slithered over rooftops, curled around gas lamps and smothered their lights to ghostly orange globes. It crawled along the riverbank, swallowing the warehouses, workhouses and tumbledown tarry-black houses that leaned over the dark water. Doors were bolted. Shutters slammed. Even the rats in the alleys froze in fright as the cloud came rolling in. The fog swallowed everything...

Ibid.: 7

After the children had read this section and highlighted, or underlined, the words which described the movement, a discussion ensued around what these words had in common. Children volunteered the idea that *the words made the fog sound like a snake or a serpent*. Another child indicated that it was a *scary monster* which scared the people in the town and this is why *doors were bolted* and *shutters slammed*. Khalid asked the children what effect they think this had on the reader and some of the children responded that it made them *picture the brown fog in my mind a bit clearer*.

Khalid introduced the term *personification* and some of the children had heard this term before and were able to describe, fairly accurately, what it was. Khalid subsequently explained the term and how it is used by writers.

Once he had given the explanation, he told the children that they would be creating their own pieces of writing which used movement in a similar way. Khalid then shared the learning intention: *I can write a description of weather using personification.* He asked the class if they thought they might be able to do this and the children gave positive and confident replies.

Khalid then shared four atmospheric images which showed mist, rain, darkness and lightning. The children were instructed to collect language to describe the movement of the meteorological phenomena. The children recalled this vocabulary from their own lexicon and augmented their lists with word banks and thesauruses. Khalid demonstrated using this language and the children created their own paragraphs with the aims of describing the weather using personification and creating a gloomy or darkening atmosphere.

The sentences created by the children included: *The darkness crept around the town and in between the houses. Lightning raced across the sky, sprinting faster than a shooting star.*

Grey clouds sneaked silently across the sky, growing darker and darker. Tumbling raindrops swirled down the windows, racing each other along gutters and ledges before diving into deep puddles.

In this lesson, the teacher skilfully led the class to recall the section of the text which he wanted the children to focus on and analyse. Rather than telling the children what they would be looking for in the text, and perhaps putting off some reluctant readers, he drew them in with the quality of the text and the rich language, in order for them to form their own conclusions about the text and the author's intentions. It was important that the task was not completed during the children's first exposure to the text but that they had enjoyed it prior to this and thus greeted the text positively, rather than something they found uninteresting. In addition to this, when children have already enjoyed the text in a group reading session, they will be of a more confident disposition when tackling any writing connected to it.

ACTIVITY 1   USING FIGURATIVE LANGUAGE TO DESCRIBE THE WEATHER

Choose a type of extreme weather to describe such as dust storm, tornado, hurricane, blizzard or flood. Create a word bank of descriptive phrases combining adjectives and nouns such as *wild wind, deafening roar* or *blinding flashes*. Then choose a type of figurative language to turn the phrases into descriptive sentences. You could choose personification, as in the case study above, or you could choose another such as simile such as *the wind was as wild as a lion hunting down its prey*, or metaphor such as *the sound of the flood was a deafening roar from a bear* or alliteration such as *the bold, blinding flashes flicked from the creepy clouds.*

- What else could be described in this way? What other forms of figurative language can be used? How could the *word bank* be built up in a different way?
- What texts can be used to support this form of descriptive writing? Could a visual stimulus be used such as incorporating film?
- How can the five senses be included in this description?

'To begin at the beginning'

With the pressures of time, it is perhaps prudent to follow the words of Dylan Thomas and look at narrative openings with the children. Of course, this is not to say that openings are where the teacher should stop. If they can establish a solid foundation that they are proud of, then they are often more inclined to extend their writing further. It is with this in mind that we 'begin at the beginning' (Thomas, 1953 [2014]: 1). Typing *how to start a story* into a search-engine will allow you to find a large number of results, each sharing a vast array of story openings. If you restrict the search to *story openers for children* then you'll still find thousands of examples and it is for this reason that we are going to focus on a manageable repertoire of effective *teachable* examples. We will examine five examples starting with *setting the scene* – a description of the world which the characters will inhabit. Then, *flashback* – an event from the past which gives the reader some insight into events that will unfurl in the story. *Prologue* – this establishes narrative context through background information, often a story occurring in a different time or place which is separate from but links to the main narrative. *In media res* – Latin for 'in the middle of things', usually describing the opening of a story which begins at a crucial point in the middle of the story rather than at the beginning. *Character description* – an introduction of the main protagonist in either the first or third person.

When *setting the scene*, Louis Sachar begins *Holes* with:

There is no lake at Camp Green Lake. There once was a very large lake here, the largest lake in Texas. That was over a hundred years ago. Now it is just a dry, flat wasteland. There used to be a town of Green Lake as well. The town shrivelled and dried up along with the lake, and the people who lived there. During the summer the daytime temperature hovers around ninety-five degrees in the shade – if you can find any shade. There's not much shade in a big dry lake.

Sachar, 2015: 3

Sachar continues to describe, in detail, what Camp Green Lake is like, taking up the first three pages of the book describing the setting and its inhabitants using carefully selected vocabulary such as *shrivelled* and *dried*.

In order for children to emulate this technique it is important that they are equipped with the language needed to describe what they can see. A vocabulary trawl may be necessary and children can find synonyms for the words that they find in the text. For *dry* they may find *arid, parched* and *scorched*, which they will be able to use to describe their own desert landscape. We as teachers should set the children the task of creating their own version of the setting, similar to that of the model. Then, later, the children can use these same techniques to create a setting description of their own for their independent narrative writing.

In Chapter 1 of *The Graveyard Book* by Neil Gaiman (2008) we see an assassin enter the house of a young family and murder them all, apart from the small toddler who luckily escapes. This is *flashback* or *time slip* to something that the man Jack did in the past,

There was a hand in the darkness, and it held a knife. The knife had a handle of polished black bone, and a blade finer and sharper than any razor. If it sliced you, you might not even know you had been cut, not immediately. The knife had done almost everything it was brought to that house to do, and both the blade and the handle were wet.

Ibid.: 2

This continues and the assassin tries to follow the toddler who luckily escapes by crawling through locked gates into a graveyard. The assassin can't get through the gates and the toddler is accepted by the graveyard ghosts who look after him. The flashback serves to inform the reader as to how the young boy, Bod, arrived at the graveyard which is where the main action of the narrative happens. This technique can be used in class in order for children to show how their character has ended up in their current setting. For example, if they have an orphaned child in their story, they may start the story with the protagonist's parents' death and then flash forward to the orphanage.

Benjamin Zephaniah (2017) uses two flashbacks at the beginning of *Refugee Boy* to show the journey that his main protagonist goes through before arriving in the UK. Justin Fisher (2017) utilises a *prologue* in *The Gold Thief* (*Ned's Circus of Marvels*). In the prologue, we witness a robbery taking place at Fort Knox in Kentucky, USA. Not only do the thieves steal all of the gold here, they also steal all of the gold reserves in the whole of America and it is a mystery as to how it happened. It also seems that there is a strange agency taking control of the situation. These strange agents have animal nicknames: Fox and Bear. The point of having this prologue is to establish a context for the rest of the story. The main character, Ned, is tasked with solving the crime later in the text. We as teachers may use this model to show children how context can be constructed so that readers understand events later in the story.

The Divine Comedy opens at line one with, 'Nel Mezzo del cammin di nostra vita' (Dante, c.1320: 1), which translates directly into English as 'Midway into the journey of our life.' This is not even the earliest example of the technique of *in media res*; we can trace it further back than the completion of Dante's masterpiece circa 1320AD and travel back through literary time and space another 2,000 years to around 750BC when Homer was utilising the technique while writing both *The Iliad* and *The Odyssey*. At the beginning of the latter, Odysseus' journey is almost at an end and the narrative is then retold through a number of flashbacks where we meet the cast of characters whom he met on his voyage. If we jump forward three millennia, there are filmmakers taking advantage of this technique from *Raging Bull* and *Raiders of the Lost Ark*, which are now a few decades old, to more modern films such as *Iron Man*, *Twelve Years a Slave* and *Ratatouille*.

In the example below, the audience are thrown into the action. There is a very short introduction to the setting and then we see the city of London chasing a small town. This opening is filled with action and makes the reader ponder what might be happening. It is a very strange concept that a city can be chasing another smaller city. This opening throws up more questions than it answers, thus inviting the reader to read on in order to find out what is happening.

> *It was a dark, blustery afternoon in spring, and the city of London was chasing a small mining town across the dried-out bed of the old North Sea. In happier times, London would never have bothered with such feeble prey. The great Traction City had once spent its days hunting far bigger towns than this, ranging north as far as the edges of the Ice Waste and south to the shores of the Mediterranean.*

> Reeve, 2015: 3

It is possible to replicate this technique in the classroom. One way of doing this is using a film sequence that is filled with action and asking the children to begin their narrative there. There are a number of short animation sequences that may be useful to use here. The short film *Replay*, which can be found on www.literacyshed.com/replay, opens *in media res*. We see a character running but we cannot see their face. The shot is cropped tight on the character's hip. We can hear that they are panting. We see that they are running across the desert towards a bunker. Once they get inside, we see their face but still we cannot identify them as they have breathing apparatus on. In the air lock, they finally remove the mask, as the air has been filtered and then the scene changes.

When using this film in the classroom, we could ask the children to complete a two-column table with the headings *what we know* and *questions*.

- *What we know*: The character is running towards a door of a bunker, across a desert.
- *Questions*: Who is she? Why is she running? Why can't she breathe the air? Does she live there? Is this in the future?

Thus we are demonstrating to the children that, when writing an opening *in media res*, the reader should be left with more questions than answers. Questions that can be answered later in their narratives.

R.J. Palacio begins with a first-person *character description* in *Wonder*. Auggie describes himself:

I KNOW I'M not an ordinary ten-year-old kid. I mean, sure, I do ordinary things. I eat ice cream. I ride my bike. I play ball. I have an XBox. Stuff like that makes me ordinary. I guess. And I feel ordinary. Inside. But I know ordinary kids don't make other ordinary kids run away screaming in playgrounds. I know ordinary kids don't get stared at wherever they go. If I found a magic lamp and I could have one wish, I would wish that I had a normal face that no one ever noticed at all.

Palacio, 2014: 1

In this description, Auggie starts off by describing how *ordinary* he is. This is followed by him saying what is extraordinary about him. This technique could be used too by children when developing other characters. For example, a superhero child may describe themselves as ordinary and doing ordinary things but then reveal later that they have super powers.

To develop a model with the children, the teacher may want to collect a list of things that children think are ordinary such attending school, riding their bike or eating ice cream and then collect a list of extraordinary superhero things such as turning invisible, being able to fly, being able to teleport to faraway places like Jupiter, lift heavy objects or move things with mind-power. This may then lead to a shared model such as:

I am just an ordinary 12-year-old. I like skateboarding in the park, I like weekends and hanging around with my friends and playing football. I eat normal food like ice cream and pizza. My teachers think I am normal; my maths teacher said I am, 'Very ordinary.' I feel most ordinary for most of the time. But there are times when I do not feel normal. Usually when I get angry or upset. Then, I feel myself changing. I can move things just by thinking about it. I can fly to the top of tall buildings and nest among the pigeons and then swoop down between the clouds. It is at these times that I am more than ordinary, I am extraordinary and I am ready to reveal my secrets.

Here we have introduced a trigger for change too. Think bananas in *Bananaman* or telephone boxes in *Superman*. It is important, with this example in mind, that reading like a writer does not always mean retelling the same story as the original narrative, but taking features that can be applied elsewhere.

In the case study below a teacher expands this activity using the same text, but in the third person instead of the first.

CASE STUDY

YEAR 3 CLASS WRITING CHARACTER DESCRIPTIONS BASED ON AUGGIE FROM *WONDER*

Melanie read the character Via's description of her younger brother Auggie to her Year 3 class. Auggie has *mandibulofacial dysostosis*, which is a medical facial deformity. This deformity was discussed with the children in previous lessons. Via's description is very detailed.

(Continued)

(Continued)

His eyes are about an inch below where they should be on his face, almost halfway down his cheeks. They slant downward at an extreme angle, almost diagonal slits that someone cut into his face, and the left one is noticeably lower than the right one. They bulge outward because his eye cavities are too shallow to accommodate them. The top eyelids are always halfway closed, like he's on the verge of sleeping. The lower eyelids sag so much they almost look like a piece of invisible string is pulling them downward: you can see the red part on the inside, like they're almost inside out. He doesn't have eyebrows or eyelashes. His nose is disproportionately big for his face, and kind of fleshy. His head is pinched in on the sides where the ears should be, like someone used giant pliers and crushed the middle part of his face. He doesn't have cheekbones. There are deep creases running down both sides of his nose to his mouth, which gives him a waxy appearance. Sometimes people assume he's been burned in a fire: his features look like they've been melted, like the drippings on the side of a candle.

Ibid.: 28

Melanie and her class analysed the language used and the structure of the descriptive paragraph step by step. She repeated the line, 'His eyes are about an inch below where they should be on his face, almost halfway down his cheeks.'

Melanie asked the children how this made them feel. Some children said they were shocked, others sad. She asked them why and was given answers like, *I feel sorry for him* and *he must be sad himself which makes me sad*. Melanie explained that the author wrote the description like this because it would first shock and then draw in the reader. She said that they would discuss more about *mandibulofacial dysostosis* in their PSHE lesson that afternoon.

Melanie then explained that what the author did was to describe each facial feature one by one in detail to build up a clear image in the reader's mind. She asked her class to remind her what an adjective was and they all knew the answer. She went on to explain that the adjectives used in Auggie's description included *big, invisible* and *giant*. She asked her class if they knew any other adjectives that the author could have used instead of these and was given answers such as *large, unseen* and *huge*.

Melanie asked the children to choose a portrait of a person from images she had previously collected and printed. They were all famous portraits but the children recognised very few of them. They included Van Gogh's self-portrait, Da Vinci's *Mona Lisa*, Sutherland's *Winston Churchill*, Vermeer's *Girl with a Pearl Earring* and Gainsborough's *Blue Boy*. The children chose one each and Melanie explained that they were going to describe their pictures in the same way that Via had described Auggie, using one feature at a time in each sentence.

The children then wrote descriptive sentences and shared with each other on the carpet which portrait they chose and how they described it.

In the case study above, the teacher focused on adjective choice. But in the selected text from *Wonder*, Palacio repeatedly uses similes such as *like a piece of invisible string is pulling them downwards* and *like someone used giant pliers and crushed the middle part of his face* and *like the drippings on the side of a candle.*

Similes are a type of figurative language which can be overused by children, but, given the right kind of guidance, they can lead to powerful descriptions as in *Wonder*. As such we can replicate the techniques used by Palacio as a model in the classroom.

ACTIVITY 2: SIMILES

Read the children *Elephant Dance* by Theresa Heine (2006). Ask the children to pick out the similes. These include, *the sun is like a ferocious tiger*, *the wind is like a wild horse* and *monsoon rains cascade from the sky like waterfalls.*

- Ask the children to think of another animal to compare to a hot sun. What animal could be compared to the wind? How can the monsoon rains be compared? Will you use an animal as with the other two similes or choose something else as in the text?
- What other similes are there in the text? How can the metaphors be used to change into similes or vice versa?
- What other books contain good examples of similes? How will you use these?

Teachers can introduce, or remind children of, the use of similes for description and model their use by introducing the children to further stimuli, such as a screen shot of the *Little Freak*, the main protagonist from this short film of the same name by Edwin Schaap. The main character in this film has similar facial deformities to those described in *Wonder*, so children can transfer the techniques displayed in the model text to a new, but similar, character before applying the practised techniques to a character they have created. This process forms a virtuous circle of skill development as illustrated below:

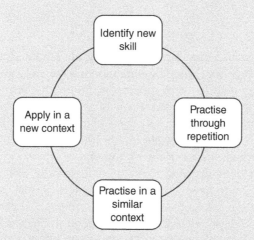

(Continued)

(Continued)

The level of independence demonstrated by children at each stage of the model will depend on the age and developmental stage of children in the cohort, although scaffolded practice of new skills will be needed by most children upon first exposure.

Early readers

Young children are able, at an early age, to internalise simple narrative structures which they can then adapt to retell their own stories. If, as Emilie Buchwald suggests, 'Children are made readers on the laps of their parents' (Buchwald, 1994, as cited in Almarzoui, 2013), then they can also be storytellers too. They can listen to and join in with simple repeated pattern stories such as *Little Red Hen* by Jerry Pinkney (2006) or *I Don't Care! Said the Bear* by Colin West (1997). In these stories, we can involve the younger children in the reading process by pausing and allowing the child to fill in a section of a repeated phrase, once they are familiar with the repetition, rhyme and rhythm of the familiar story.

A popular book of this genre is *Brown Bear, Brown Bear, What Do You See?* by Bill Martin Jr and Eric Carle (1997). The opening is as follows:

Brown bear, brown bear what do you see?

I see a red bird looking at me.

Red bird, red bird what do you see?

I see a yellow duck looking at me.

Yellow duck, yellow duck what do you see?

Ibid.: 1

The pattern continues with a number of other brightly coloured animals. Children enjoy following the pattern and *reading along* by remembering the story and linking the images to the words that have been read to them repeatedly. Some children also enjoy adding their own characters to the story to retell *Brown Bear, Brown Bear, What Do You See?*, with additional strangely coloured creatures such as *purple chicken* or *shiny pig*. This is a very early version of *reading* like a writer and developing the outcomes which we desire for our children as they advance through their journey as authors.

Teachers of younger children may wish to point out features of writing in simple story books to the children. By highlighting these features in the sentences, such as capital letters and full stops, then we are using the books to develop early writing. We can also point out simple describing words such as *big* or *small* and draw attention to colours and then replicate their uses in model sentences. This will enable the children to emulate these techniques as they begin to write their own sentences. Young children may reproduce these sentences, changing very little, but they are actively practising techniques ready to use, independently, later.

As children become more confident readers, they will be able to identify increasing numbers of features in the stories that they are reading; however, most learners will need these pointing out to them and modelled a number of times before they can use them effectively.

Once children begin to use simple structures, such as expanded noun phrases and complete simple sentences, they can begin to create their own simple narratives. Novice writers may want to describe a character in very simple terms: for example, *the fat man* or *the angry boy*. Model texts can be used to demonstrate how authors describe a character effectively.

Teachers who would like their students to emulate this technique need to provide further text-based examples for their students to analyse and then reproduce. Once they have carried this activity out effectively, then students can use the technique to create descriptions of their own characters. Teachers can scaffold this technique in order to enable all children to create their own description. The teacher may wish to provide images of characters which the children can describe using this technique. One character, who has a face full of interesting features, is the Old Crone from Disney's *Snow White* (1937). In the case study below a Reception class teacher uses this image to produce some oral and written descriptions.

CASE STUDY

RECEPTION CLASS WRITING DESCRIPTIONS BASED ON *SNOW WHITE'S* OLD CRONE

Mia, a Reception class teacher, showed the children an image of the Old Crone. The children were animated in their response and Mia asked them why. Some told her it was because of her eyes, but others said it was her nose, chin, hair and mouth. She asked the children to describe each prominent feature: her eyes, chin, nose, fingers, clothes, hair, teeth and mouth.

Mia then wrote the words they used onto a board. She sounded each word phonetically as she wrote. The words included *big*, *ugly*, *bad*, *mean*, *evil* and *horrible*. Mia asked the class if they had ever heard of an Old Crone. None had; she then asked what they would call this character. Everyone agreed that she was a witch. Mia asked the children to help her draw a witch face on the board next to the adjectives she had scribed. She chose one child at a time to add each feature listed earlier, but also asked them to add *angry* eyebrows, *large* warts and *pointy* hairs.

She gave her class paper plates and asked them to design their own witch masks. Once completed, the children gathered on the carpet again. Mia read the words collected from earlier and asked her class to choose their favourites. She then asked the children to write these favourites on the back of the plates. She supported a group of children while her teaching assistant supported the less able. The masks and words were then shared on the carpet.

The teacher delivered this lesson in the autumn term. Not all of her class were confident writers, but writing was celebrated and encouraged in the classroom. Among the choosing stations were mark-making and writing-based independent activities, both inside and outside the classroom. This helped to encourage a positive attitude towards whole-class writing activities as in the case study above.

ACTIVITY 3   GATHERING FUEL FOR WRITING

Choose an image for a character. Ask children to create descriptive spidergrams, adjective wheels or word webs to gather vocabulary. Then ask them to select those words which precisely describe the features of the character; generate some model sentences which are similar in structure to the text models which the class have been analysing. For example, *The witch's cruel and devious eyes bulged in their sockets. Her hair hung limp and grey around her bony shoulders.*

Once the model sentences have been produced, in discussion with the children, develop a class model through the process of shared writing.

- What image will you use? How can this activity be adapted to describe a setting? What type of device will you use to gather the words necessary for describing?
- How can this activity be extended? What can be used to encourage more independent writing?

FOCUS ON RESEARCH

The Education Endowment Foundation's meta-analysis of research on improving literacy at KS2 (EEF, 2017: 8) identified the importance of developing children's language and found that:

> *Reading to pupils and discussing books is still important for this age group. Exposing pupils to an increasingly wide range of texts, with an appropriate level of challenge, will develop their language capability. This should include active engagement with a wide range of genres and media, including digital texts. This variation is likely to be motivating and engaging and it provides an opportunity to explicitly teach the features and structures of different types of text, which can develop more advanced comprehension and reasoning skills.*

Conclusion

High-quality texts are essential in the teaching of reading for writing. These texts need to be shared and analysed, dissected and scrutinised, considered and questioned, evaluated and explored. The children should be immersed in a narrative so that they feel able to write a narrative. They need to read widely, from a range of authors and a range of genres. They need to experience, and compare, how characters are described, how characterisation is built, how setting and atmosphere are created. They need to explore how narratives open, what makes an effective ending, how authors build suspense and tension and also how moments of quiet are written. They also need to learn how an author uses action within a narrative.

By immersing children into narratives we help them to look beyond the words and learn how to infer and deduce the information woven into the plot by the author. Children need us to help them to look at the precision of the vocabulary and how a word can hold so much power within a sentence. It is only when they are doing all of these things, and much more, that children can begin to explore using it in their own writing. It is essential, therefore, that we read a wide range of texts in order to support the writing of our pupils. It does take time and effort to build up a good repertoire of books each year, but there are also fantastic people on social media who share books and how they have used them in class. As teachers, we want to teach our young writers to be brave and creative, to know the *rules* but not always be bound by them. We want children to feel scaffolded enough in their learning to feel confident in making their own *authorly* decisions. Ultimately, reading unlocks the door to writing. As teachers, we need to ensure that every child is given the key.

Further reading

The following texts provide guidance on making links between reading and writing:

Barrs, M. and Cork, V. (2001) *The Reader in the Writer: The Links Between the Study of Literature and Writing Development at KS2*. London: CLPE.

Bushnell, A. and Waugh, D. (eds) (2017) *Inviting Writing Across the Curriculum*. London: Sage.

Chamberlain, L., with Kerrigan-Draper, E. (2016) *Inspiring Writing in Primary Schools*. London: Sage.

Martin, T., Lovat, C. and Purnell, G. (2004) *The Really Useful Literacy Book. Being Creative with Literacy in the Primary Classroom*. London: Routledge: Falmer. Chapter 11: 'Where did our writing come from? Exploring the writing process'.

Recommended websites

Love Reading 4 Kids – www.lovereading4kids.co.uk (accessed 8 June 2018).

Replay animation – www.literacyshed.com/replay (accessed 8 June 2018).

Little Freak animation – https://www.literacyshed.com/the-thinking-shed.html (accessed 20 May 2018).

References

Almarzoui, A. (2013) *Lifelong readers are born 'on the laps of their parents'* https://www.goodreads.com/quotes/9274-children-are-made-readers-on-the-laps-of-their-parents (accessed on 8 June 2018).

Cremin, T., Mottram, M., Collins, F., Powell, S. and Safford, K. (2009) Teachers as readers: building communities of readers. *Literacy* 43(1): 11–19.

Dante, A. (c.1320) *The Divine Comedy. From Mapping Dante: A Study of Places in the Commedia.* https://www.mappingdante.com/inferno/ (accessed 4 May 2018).

DfE (2013) *The national curriculum in England: Key stages 1 and 2 framework document.* London: DfE.

EEF (Education Endowment Foundation) (2017). *Improving Literacy in Key Stage Two.* London: Education Endowment Foundation.

Fisher, J. (2017) *The Gold Thief (Ned's Circus of Marvels,* Book 2*).* London: Harper Collins Children's.

Gaiman, N. (2008) *The Graveyard Book.* London: Bloomsbury, Children's Education Edition.

Heine, T. (2006) *Elephant Dance.* London: Barefoot Books.

Lloyd Jones, R. (2013) *Wild Boy.* London: Candlewick Press.

Martin Jr, B. and Carle, E. (1997) *Brown Bear, Brown Bear, What Do You See?* London: Puffin.

Ontario (2003) *Early Reading Strategy – The Report of the Expert Panel on Early Reading in Ontario.* Available at: www.edu.gov.on.ca (Ontario Ministry of Education) (accessed 12 June 2018).

Palacio, R.J. (2014) *Wonder.* London: Corgi Children's.

Pinkney, J. (2006) *The Little Red Hen.* London: Dial Books.

Prose, F. (2012) *Reading Like a Writer: A Guide for People Who Love Books and for Those Who Want to Write Them.* Knoxville, TN: Union Books.

Reeve, P, (2015) *Mortal Engines (Predator Cities).* London: Scholastic.

Thomas, D. (2014) *Under Milk Wood: The Definitive Edition.* London: W&N.

Sachar, L. (2015) *Holes.* London: Bloomsbury.

West, C. (1997) *I Don't Care! Said the Bear.* London: Walker Books.

Zephaniah, B. (2017) *Refugee Boy.* London: Bloomsbury.

3

SCAFFOLDING WRITING

TEACHERS' STANDARDS

This chapter will help you with the following Teachers' Standards:

4. **Plan and teach well-structured lessons**
   - impart knowledge and develop understanding through effective use of lesson time;
   - promote a love of learning and children's intellectual curiosity;
   - contribute to the design and provision of an engaging curriculum within the relevant subject area(s).

5. **Adapt teaching to respond to the strengths and needs of all pupils**
   - know when and how to differentiate appropriately, using approaches which enable pupils to be taught effectively;
   - have a secure understanding of how a range of factors can inhibit pupils' ability to learn, and how best to overcome these.

KEY QUESTIONS

- What do we mean by a writing scaffold?
- How can teachers make the writing process more accessible?
- Which writing processes can we scaffold?
- When is the right time to scaffold writing?
- How much is too much?
- How can we vary the range of scaffolds that we use?

Introduction

Much of the reasoning behind *scaffolding* learning in the classroom has its roots in Vygotsky's work (for example, 1978) and, later, in the work of Bruner (for example, 1985). These writers believed that when beginning new learning children needed support from teachers or other experts. Vygotsky's ideas are encapsulated in the *Zone of Proximal Development* which, put simply, is the difference between what a child can do without help and what he or she can achieve with the intervention and support of an expert (see also Chapters 1 and 5). Thus, scaffolding emerges when additional aid or support is needed for a child to experience success in the field. In a blog, Didau (2015) offers the conclusion that 'pretty much everyone thinks that scaffolding students' work is a "good thing"' and provides two principles for the effective use of scaffolding:

1. We should never use scaffolding to make work easier.
2. Never put up scaffolding unless you have a plan to take it down.

These are good principles to follow because if work is too difficult to complete then perhaps it is the incorrect task for those pupils and if scaffolds are left in place for too long then children may become over reliant on them.

However, which part of the writing process should be scaffolded? We can break the whole process of writing down into three stages.

1. Pre-writing
2. Writing
3. Post-writing

Certain aspects of each stage can have scaffolds applied. The pre-writing stage, in which skills and structures are taught, is probably the most important and the stage that can take the longest time. Within this stage there are a number of important factors for the writer, and therefore the teacher, to take into consideration. First, the ideas – what to write about and how. Then, the words used in order to describe or explain the initial ideas and the structure of both the sentences; then the overall text structure, including where to start, what to include and how to end.

Ideas scaffolding happens in most writing lessons. Rarely do teachers instruct their pupils to write without scaffolding their ideas first. This is usually done through a variety of stimuli, including props, text, film and images. Once the stimulus has been chosen, then the pre-write or preparing to write stage can begin. Talk is important at this point in order for the children to share their ideas about the stimulus. For example, if an image is used, like the one below, teachers can use questioning to elicit ideas about the narrative.

In the case study below, a Year 3 class use this same image to produce a piece of writing guided by the scaffolding process as modelled by their teacher.

Image 3.1 This image can be found online here:

https://pixabay.com/en/fantasy-fairytale-elve-old-man-owl-1481583/

CASE STUDY

YEAR 3 CLASS USING AN IMAGE AND PROPS TO CREATE A CHARACTER DESCRIPTION

Ellen, a Year 3 teacher, gathered her class on the carpet and showed them the image above. She asked the class to work in *talk partners* to discuss what they thought of the character. While the children were discussing the image, Ellen wrote the following prompts on the board:

Who is he going to find?

What does he keep in his bag?

Where has he been?

When did he get his owl?

Why does he have the symbol of a tree?

She then read these questions to the class and asked the children to continue to discuss the character with their partners. Ellen then asked the children what they thought he might have had in his bag. She got answers that included *food, medicine,*

(Continued)

(Continued)

water, weapons and *bird seed.* She then showed the children a leather satchel similar to the one in the image. She opened it slowly and produced a key, an egg and a purple jewel. She asked the children to discuss with each other what the objects were for. These ideas were discussed and elaborated upon. For example, when the children told Ellen that the key was for a chest, she asked the children what was inside the chest and where it was kept. When the children told her that the egg was the owl's baby, she asked the children how he keeps it warm and when it will hatch. When the children told her the purple jewel was from the queen she asked them why she had given it to him and what did he do to earn it.

After more discussion Ellen wrote the following sentence starters on the board:

The elf was going to . . .
He had to go and visit . . .
In his backpack was . . .
He carried a . . .
On his belt was an image of a tree because . . .

Then she added less scaffolded sentence starters such as:

The elf . . .
He was . . .
He went . . .
On his . . .
His owl . . .

The children then wrote their character description using either set of sentence starters or they could write independently. Most children used the scaffolded sentence starters as prompts but then wrote their own independent sentences once they had got started.

The children then shared their writing with each other on the carpet.

In the case study, there was very little differentiation yet the outcome varied vastly. The teacher supported the less able by modelling full sentences on a whiteboard which the children could use to get them started. The more able still used the scaffolded sentence prompts but quickly moved on to independent writing without being asked to do so. The sentence starters worked as confidence builders to their writing.

ACTIVITY 1   USING IMAGES TO SCAFFOLD WRITING

Share an image like the one used in the case study and ask the children to discuss what they think the answers are to the '5W' questions. The 5 Ws are:

- Who?
- What?
- Where?
- When?
- Why?

The first time that this is done some of the children may find it difficult to come up with suitable answers. You may want to ask other questions as prompts such as *Do you think the character suits the name . . .? Why?* Ask additional questions to add details such as *What do you think he has in his pockets and belt pouches? What could we call the town? What special abilities does the owl have?*
All responses could be recorded in order to be used in a shared write.

Scaffolding vocabulary

While discussing the stimulus, it is important that we as teachers develop a discussion around the language that can be used to describe the characters, the landscape and, ultimately, narrate the story, as in the case study above. Depending on their lexicon, scaffolding may be required in order for the children to accurately describe what they can see in the picture or film stimulus. This may be done through teacher or peer discussion. In the image above vocabulary development may take place so that gloves can become gauntlets, stick becomes a staff and the castle becomes a citadel. It is important that children receive multiple exposures to this higher-register language in order for them to use it in a range of contexts. Word banks and thesauruses may also be used to scaffold the vocabulary, although children need to be taught how to use these correctly.

For example, if describing a forest then children may be given a word bank containing adjectives:

- majestic
- vermilion
- gloomy
- shadowy
- spidery
- spiky
- mysterious
- gnarled.

Unless children know what each of these words means, and how it can be used in context, then the list is ineffective. It is necessary to discuss and explain the meaning of each word. Beck et al. (2013) recommend that words and definitions are explained in 'everyday language' to make them 'accessible so students can understand the concept with ease' (ibid.: 46). They further explain that some definitions can be confusing to some students, who will then use the word erroneously. One example that Beck et al. (2013) use is *disrupt*, with the definition *to break up* or *split*. This could be misinterpreted by the children to mean physically breaking something up, as in *we disrupted the candy bar so we could all share it*. A more child-friendly explanation may be to define disrupt as *rudely interrupting something* or *causing a problem which will stop something occurring*. Simple definitions for the words in the list above would be *majestic: beautiful and impressive* or *vermilion: a bright red colour* etc.

Once simple definitions have been established, it is possible to reinforce them by asking simple questions. For example, *which of the following would more likely to be described as vermilion:*

- blood or soil?
- the setting sun or a raven?
- a sports car or a tree?

Or,

Which of the following may be described as majestic: an old oak tree, a palace, a deck chair, piglets or a mountain?

In the case study below, a Year 6 class use a *Descriptosaurus* by Alison Wilcox (2013) to help them use more advanced vocabulary with scaffolded support.

CASE STUDY

YEAR 6 CLASS DESCRIBING A JUNGLE USING A *DESCRIPTOSAURUS*

The Year 6 class had used the *Descriptosaurus* many times before and were used to the term to *magpie* ideas from it. Lynne, their teacher, used the 2nd edition from 2013 that includes a CD-ROM so as to display the text from the book onto the interactive whiteboard. The topic the class had been studying in Geography was Extreme Environments and Lynne had been using the topic in her writing lessons.

She began by showing images of jungles from South America, Vietnam, Kauai and India. Each jungle was discussed in small groups. The children were given whiteboards and pens. Lynne then clicked on the CD link to the *Descriptosaurus* website. She selected *Settings* then *Landscapes, Forest and Woods* and, finally, *Words*. Displayed on the board were groups of *Nouns* including *trunks, branches, roots, canopy, vines* and *creepers*. Lynne asked the children to copy three nouns of their choice. *Adjectives* were also displayed, including *vast, towering, impenetrable, barbed, gnarled* and *decaying.* Lynne asked the children to copy three adjectives of their choice too. Then she showed *Verbs* which included *tangled, stretched, arched, writhed, swayed* and *shrouded.* Three of these were selected by the children and written on the whiteboards. Lynne then showed the *Descriptosaurus* example sentences where *nouns, adjectives* and *verbs* had been blended together such as: 'The branches of the thick, tangled trees had spread and twisted to form dark, overhead tunnels and created secret paths. Like some prehistoric beast, the huge, twisted limbs of the tree guarded the entrance' (ibid.: 8).

Lynne highlighted how, in these two sentences, the word *twisted* had been used both times in different ways. She asked the class for an adjective that they had picked and a child told her that she had picked *gnarled.* Lynne then wrote the following two sentences as a model: *The gnarled trees were vast and towering. Impenetrable vines stretched over the gnarled branches.*

The children then used their own selected nouns, adjectives and verbs to write their own descriptions of a jungle.

The *Descriptosaurus* is a DfE-recommended resource that is all about scaffolding writing. The class were used to using it previously and the teacher had used the other versions of it in different genres of writing. The other versions are *Descriptosaurus: Action and Adventure, Descriptosaurus: Fantasy, Descriptosaurus: Ghost Stories* and *Descriptosaurus: Myths and Legends.*

ACTIVITY 2   EXTENDING DESCRIPTIONS WITH THE *DESCRIPTOSAURUS*

Ask the children to *magpie* words from the *Descriptosaurus* in a similar way to the case study, but include adverbs from *Part Four: Additional Vocabulary Development.* In this same section there are *Connectives* (meaning *Conjunctions*) which can be used as sentence starters to scaffold writing too.

- How else can the *Descriptosaurus* be used? How can the text be differentiated for younger writers? How can the more able use the book to extend their writing?
- How can the *Adverbs* be changed into *Adjectives*? What other adverbs can be used that do not end in *–ly*?

Look at *Part Two: Characters* in the *Descriptosaurus* and use both the *Appearance* and *Emotions and Personality* sections to describe not characters but settings.

(Continued)

(Continued)

- How can this teach children about personification? What other types of figurative language can the *Descriptosaurus* help children understand?
- How can the other sections of the book be used?

Bruner (1985) maintained that the learner passes through mental developmental phases, which are supported by structured learning experiences. Bruner argued that speech is a primary mechanism for thought, and therefore it is vitally important for children to have the opportunity to talk through their ideas. Bruner called the support that adults provide in the learning process 'scaffolding', whereby an adult varies the level of support, gradually withdrawing it as the child gains in competency (see Waugh et al., 2017: 21).

Scaffolding sentences

If a text is being used as a stimulus for writing, then challenging vocabulary may be scaffolding through pre-teaching. *The Dream Snatcher* by Abi Elphinstone opens with a prologue:

*There are footprints in the snow, **sunken** marks **picked out** by the moonlight. They **weave** a path through the forest, round the ring of ancient oak trees and on towards the wooden hut. But there they stop, and the smoke curling out of the chimney is the only sign that anyone is inside.*

*Seven **cloaked figures** sit round a table, their hoods pulled up despite the fire crackling in the **grate**. At first, they whisper together, their voices low and guarded. And then the whispers fade, heads drop and lips curl back. A **chant** begins. There are no words, just grunted sounds scratching at the back of throats.*

One of the figures pushes back her hood and long grey hair falls about her shoulders.

Ibid.: 1

This book is recommended for children aged around eight or nine, which means that the vocabulary could be challenging for some. The words in bold are not usually highlighted but have been highlighted here to show that these words may present a challenge for children of this age. It would aid some children if they had been taught the meaning of these unfamiliar words prior to reading them in the text. Beck et al. (2013) identify language in a *three tier system*. The *first tier* are words that children will learn through their normal everyday lives and interactions. Words such as *mum, play, school, lunch* and so on. *Tier two* words are academic words which children will encounter usually through written language. These words are more sophisticated than the everyday language used by the children; however, they represent concepts that the children can understand and 'explain these words using words that are already well known to them' (ibid.: 25). For example, in the passage above the words in bold have been selected as they would be categorised as *tier two* words for some eight year olds. The criterion for the tiers is flexible and what constitutes a *tier two* word for one child may not be a *tier two* word for others. These are words which children may have already encountered but are unlikely to use in their everyday language or in this specific context. To illustrate this, take the word *sunken*. The children may have encountered this word in the context of shipwrecks or pirate treasure but not as an adjective for eyes or the depression of footprints in snow. Once the word had been explained by the teacher, then children would be able to explain it in their own words. Beck et al. (ibid.) describe a *third tier* of words as words which are very specialised and specific to a topic. For example, *portcullis* is only ever going to be used when describing a castle. In science lessons words such as *conical flask* or *ovule* are technical and do not cross several subject domains in the way a *tier two* word such as *majestic* would.

Once ideas are in place and writing is going to begin, we will want to develop the children's skills at the sentence level. Sentences are the currency in which writers deal. Words are important, but how they are placed within sentences can have a huge effect on the reader. When a text is used as a stimulus for writing it is possible to select sentences to demonstrate specific techniques such as using a rhetorical questioning, repetition for effect or metaphors for detailed description. When the specific structure is introduced, then we can encourage children to imitate it in order to practise that writing technique. Myhill et al. describe the process of imitation as 'a powerful tool to support initial learning about a text' (2016: 6).

Cressida Cowell (2017) describes a dark forest at the beginning of her book *The Wizards of Once* as follows:

Perhaps you feel that you know what a dark forest looks like.

Well, I can tell you right now that you don't. These were forests darker than you would believe possible, darker than inkspots, darker than midnight, darker than space itself, and as twisted and as tangled as a Witch's heart.

Ibid.: 30

There are two main teaching points here:

• the use of the first-person narrator addressing the reader directly;
• the use of repeated similes to describe the darkness of the forest.

Both of these structures could be imitated by children. Myhill et al. (2016: 7) explain that 'imitation is not the same as copying – it involves some kind of re-creation of grammatical patterns or ideas, rather than a direct duplication'. It allows children to experiment with language within the given structures. Imitating also allows children to practise new skills and experiment with the structure even when they may be unable to explain the device grammatically. Myhill et al. also assert that this method helps 'to embed new structures cognitively within the student's writing repertoire' (ibid.). It allows them to experience success in their own writing, as can be seen in the case study below.

CASE STUDY

YEAR 4 CLASS USING DIRECT IMITATION FROM *THE WIZARDS OF ONCE* TO WRITE DESCRIPTIVE SENTENCES

Jamal, a Year 4 teacher, read the opening from *The Wizards of Once* (Cowell, 2017). He had the passage above photocopied for the children and the children were then asked to read this again independently. He asked the children what they thought of the descriptions and if they noticed any techniques the author had used that they were familiar with. The children immediately spotted the repeated use of similes as they had been learning about this in previous lessons. Jamal then asked which their favourite was and most replied that *witch's heart* was their preferred simile.

Jamal also highlighted the structure of the writing including the use of *darker* three times. He asked the children to suggest different similes for darkness. The children first worked in small groups and then shared with the rest of the class. Jamal then demonstrated, through shared writing, how this same structure could be taken and used by the children. The example he wrote was:

These were forests ~~darker than you would believe possible~~, darker than ~~inkspots~~,

These were forests so dark you would think it was impossible, darker than a bear's cave

darker than ~~midnight~~, darker than ~~space itself~~, and as twisted and as ~~tangled~~ as a ~~Witch's heart~~.

darker than a raven's wing, darker than the far corner of the universe, as twisted as an ancient wizard's gnarled fingers.

The children then wrote their own version on whiteboards following the same structure. This was then shared and peers suggested improvements each other's writing. Once edited and improved, the children wrote in their books. Jamal asked them to add additional sentences if they had completed this, mimicking the same style of the author. The more able did this independently and Jamal supported the rest of the class where necessary. Finally, the descriptions were shared with the class on the carpet.

In the case study, the teacher used a very short extract which was only three sentences long. This seemed to work to good effect as it was a long and daunting text for the children to use. They directly imitated the style of the author but used their own ideas to develop independent descriptions. Direct imitation is something which can help children to find their own written voice. It is by imitating other authors that we find the style in which we are most comfortable to write.

ACTIVITY 3   DIRECT IMITATION

After the children have experimented with the direct imitation then they can apply this method to some independent writing. Provide some stimulus such as an image, film or props. Perhaps use something which includes colour so that the scene can be described using adjectives similar to dark, such as gloomy, spooky, mysterious etc. For example, *The city was gloomier than you could ever imagine, gloomier than a bleak winter's day, gloomier than a mist-filled graveyard, gloomier than the saddest face and as cold as an iceberg-filled ocean.*

- Which images, film or props could you use for the children to describe? Which other text extracts can be used in a similar way to the case study above?
- What length of extract will you use? How can you extend the activity to inspire further writing opportunities?

DADWAVERS

Once a number of sentence structures have been practised then children can use them with increased confidence in their writing. Perhaps one way to encourage this is to give children a list of criteria that you want them to include – for example, the use of repeated similes, directly addressing the reader or use of a range of interesting vocabulary etc. However, these criteria often rely on the children remembering which sentence structures to use. It may be prudent therefore to list the sentence structures that you would like children to use. One way of doing this is to use DADWAVERS. This mnemonic was developed by the teachers who created The Literacy Shed and can be used in a variety of ways to scaffold sentence openings. DADWAVERS stands for:

- Description
- Action
- Dialogue
- Where
- Adverb
- Verb
- Estimation of time
- Rhetorical question
- Simile or metaphor.

The basic premise is that children should aim to include each of the above features as close to the beginning of their sentences as possible.

Description – These are sentences which describe settings or characters.

Action – This focuses on the movement within the scene and will contain a number of verbs so that the reader gets a sense of that motion.

Dialogue – This helps children to remember to include speech. Dialogue may be missed out when scaffolding techniques such as DADWAVERS are not used. This part can be left out when creating a descriptive setting which has no characters within it. Or perhaps the dialogue is directly to the reader.

Where – These sentences begin with an adverbial of place and anchor the sentence in a particular place.

Adverb – Adverbial sentences are those which start with a fronted adverbial.

Verb – This is a sentence which has a verb as the header.

Estimation of time – These sentences begin with an adverbial of time. They do not always include a specific time though; they can include some of the language of time such as *after a few minutes, seconds ticked by* or they can suggest a time – for example, *as the sun went down* or *as twilight settled across the sky*.

Rhetorical questions – These address the reader and invite them to think about sections of the story. Examples could include questions such as *have you ever been lost in the dark?* or *have you ever wondered what you would do if you came face to face with a dragon?*

Simile or metaphor – Any figurative language could be used here. These sentences describe a section of the narrative using imagery.

In order for children to be able to use this, they will need to know how to construct sentences which fit into each criterion – for example, using prepositional language at the beginning of the *where* sentence like *Behind the tree stood a figure* or *In the sky, the sun shone*. Similarly, when writing a *simile/metaphor* sentence, the writer must understand what is meant by the figurative terminology in order to be successful.

In the case study below, a Year 5 teacher uses DADWAVERS as a scaffolding device in their writing.

CASE STUDY

YEAR 5 CLASS USING SCAFFOLDING TECHNIQUES INCLUDING *DADWAVERS* TO DESCRIBE A WINTER LANDSCAPE

Rosy, a Year 5 teacher, had prepared the classroom prior to the lesson opening. The image below was displayed on the interactive whiteboard. The image's wintry landscape was linked loosely to the text that the class were studying, C.S. Lewis' *The Lion, The Witch and The Wardrobe*, in order to allow the children to transfer their previous learning and apply it to their writing.

Noun	Adjective
Verb	Adverb

Image 3.2   This image can be found on pixabay here:

https://pixabay.com/en/snow-fairy-tale-christmas-forest-1911798/

Rosy asked for a definition for each quadrant heading and established the correct meaning with some examples from the image. Then the children were given 15 minutes to fill the four quadrants. While the children were collecting the language, Rosy assessed their knowledge of these four word classes by seeing where there were gaps. If there were gaps she supported during the 15 minutes. Once the children had exhausted their own ideas, they were asked to move around the room to share and swap language to fill their grid.

Rosy then regrouped the children and synonyms for some of the words were discussed. She asked the children to write a single sentence on whiteboards which described an aspect of the image. Many of the sentences were simple *article – noun – verb* sentences with varying degrees of description and all followed a similar structure: *The cold, white snow covered the ground. The cold, dark night was lit up by the bright windows. The tall trees surrounded the snowy ground.*

Rosy pointed out that there was some repetition in the structures and singled out those with different sentence structures for praise. She then asked if the children knew of other ways in which they could start sentences or create sentences. The children volunteered a few vague structures before the teacher revealed the DADWAVERS list. She went through each part clarifying meaning and defining each one for the children, sometimes with examples if they were unclear.

(Continued)

(Continued)

The children were then given large post-it notes and asked to add sentences describing the image on the board to each of the pre-prepared large A2 sheets. The children were challenged to add as many as they could to each sheet as long as they had at least one example on each.

After another 15 minutes Rosy asked the children to stop adding to the collection and read all of the sentences on the sheets. The children were then encouraged to add comments around the post-it note sentences that they particularly liked. Some added stars, ticks and smiley face symbols to show their appreciation of favourites. Following this activity, Rosy scaffolded the process further by selecting an example from each of the sheets. She talked about the editing process and how they might use the sentences within their writing.

The children had written sentences such as:

D   *Crisp, white, deep snow covered the ground and shimmered in the Arctic moonlight.*

A   *The snow fell harder, flurries swirled all around making it almost impossible to see.*

D   *'We are nearly there buddy. Come on you can do it!' he called to the person trailing behind.*

W   *At the edge of the clearing, two figures stumbled from the trees.*

A   *Slowly, the two tired men made their way towards the lights shining in the clearing.*

V   *Placing one foot purposefully in front of the other, they slogged through the snow which was up to their thighs.*

E   *It felt like hours had passed and still the house seemed no closer.*

R   *Will we make it? he thought to himself. He thought he would but he was worried about his partner.*

S   *The old fisherman's hut sat in the middle of the frozen lake like a lighthouse filled with the warmth that they greatly needed.*

The children then worked independently to create their own paragraph using DADWAVERS to help scaffold their sentences. Some examples of their favourite sentences were then shared on the carpet.

The children had not used *DADWAVERS* before, but had a good understanding of the terminology of each part. This contributed to the successful writing that the children achieved.

It is important that *DADWAVERS* are introduced at the right time in the classroom and may need adapting slightly for particular year groups to understand the concepts.

ACTIVITY 4   USING *DADWAVERS*

Develop your own version of DADWAVERS – for example, change it to a non-fiction version, such as:

- decide who it's for
- articulate formally
- description
- where/what/when/why (+how)
- adverbs
- verbs
- explanation
- rhetorical repetition
- summary.

You could also ask children to use it as a checklist for their writing where they tick the boxes of the feature they have remembered to include.

Assessment

D ☐

A ☐

D ☐

W ☐

A ☐

V ☐

E ☐

R ☐

S ☐

- How else can DADWAVERS be adapted? What parts will you change and what parts will you keep the same?
- How can DADWAVERS be differentiated for younger children? How can it be used to challenge more able pupils?

DADWAVERS AS SCAFFOLDS

At first glance, this activity may seem like all creativity is sucked out of the writing process in favour of a very rigid structure; however, there are no hard and fast rules in using DADWAVERS. They can be used, as in the example above, in order to create a single paragraph or they can be used as sentence scaffolds to insert into a longer piece to add variation.

A further challenge can be used to encourage the children to think creatively by constraining their choices. If, for example, you challenge the children to write a DADWAVERS paragraph that follows DADWAVERS in order, then they will have to write each sentence with more thought. As suggested by Stokes (2006), 'constraints promote creativity by enforcing rules which they need to follow. Whereas when people are given a free rein to solve a problem, they tend to be wholly uncreative and they focus on 'what's worked well in the past' (ibid.: 11).

There are other ways of scaffolding paragraphs in this way such as *slow writing*, developed by David Didau (2014) or *sentence stacking* by Jane Considine (2016) (see Further reading).

Conclusion

When introducing a new writing skill to children, teachers should consider how this might need to be scaffolded. In most cases the level of challenge to the task should not be altered, rather we should vary the tools we give the children, so that they can be successful. Scaffolds are to be used when necessary and appropriate but not all of the time, as this can lead to some children becoming overly dependent on the scaffolds in place. As pointed out by Didau (2015), scaffolds 'shouldn't be erected without a plan to remove them'. Once the children can effectively use the skill with the scaffold, remove or reduce the amount of scaffolding and wait to see how the children respond. It is also fair to say that this is not a *one size fits all* process. What works for one child may need to be adapted for another pupil. Scaffolding supports for English as an additional language (EAL) children or for children with additional needs will also need further consideration.

Further reading

DADWAVERS – https://www.literacyshedblog.com/dadwavers/dadwavers

For slow writing:

Didau, D. (2014) *The Secret of Literacy: Making the Implicit Explicit.* Carmarthen: Independent Thinking Press.

For sentence stacking:

Considine, J. (2016) *The Write Stuff: Transforming the Teaching of Writing*. Kettering: The Training Space.

References

Beck, I., McKeown, M. and Kucan, L. (2013) *Bringing Words to Life: Robus Vocabulary Instruction* (2nd edition). New York: Guildford Press (Kindle edition, accessed 5 May 2018).

Bruner, J.S. (1985) Vygotsky: a historical and conceptual perspective, in Wertsch, J. (ed.), *Culture, Communication and Cognition: Vygotskian Perspectives*. Cambridge: Cambridge University Press: 21–34.

Cowell, C. (2017) *The Wizards of Once*. London: Hodder and Stoughton (Kindle edition, accessed 15 May 2018).

Didau, D. (2015) *Scaffolding: What can we Learn from the Metaphor?* http://www.learningspy.co.uk/literacy/scaffolding-what-we-can-learn-from-the-metaphor/ (accessed 12 May 2018).

Elphinstone, A. (2015) *The Dream Snatcher*. London: Simon and Schuster Children's.

Myhill, D., Jones, S., Watson, A. and Lines, L. (2016) *Essential Primary Grammar*. Oxford: Oxford University Press.

Stokes, P. (2006) *Creativity from Constraints: The Psychology of Breakthrough*. London: Springer.

Vygotsky, L.S. (1978) *Mind in Society: The Development of Higher Psychological Processes*. Cambridge, MA: Harvard University Press.

Waugh, D, Jolliffe, W. and Allott, K. (eds) (2017) *Primary English for Trainee Teachers*. London: Sage.

Wilcox, A. (2013) *Descriptosaurus* (2nd edition). London: Routledge.

4

WRITING FOR CHILDREN

TEACHERS' STANDARDS

This chapter will help you with the following Teachers' Standard:

3. Demonstrate good subject and curriculum knowledge:
    - have a secure knowledge of the relevant subject(s) and curriculum areas, foster and main-
      tain pupils' interest in the subject, and address misunderstandings;
    - demonstrate a critical understanding of developments in the subject and curriculum areas,
      and promote the value of scholarship;
    - demonstrate an understanding of and take responsibility for promoting high standards of
      literacy, articulacy and the correct use of Standard English, whatever the teacher's special-
      ist subject.

KEY QUESTIONS

- What are the benefits of writing for children?
- Which strategies enable successful writing for children?
- How can children's writing benefit from engaging with their teachers' writing?

Introduction

Why would teachers write for children when there are thousands of published stories already?

When did you last write a poem? When did you last ask children to write poetry? For many teachers, the answer to the first question is probably *when I was training as a teacher* or *when I attended a course*. Their answer to the second question would probably be *recently*, since teachers frequently expect children to write in a range of forms. Of course, there are many wonderful texts which can be used to show children a range of genres, but there are also many reasons why creating our own texts can be beneficial. In this chapter, we will examine some of the reasons why it is important that teachers of writing are also writers themselves. These might include:

- If you write, you show children that you value writing and that writing is not just something they have to do because they are pupils.
- You provide a model of writing which children can attempt to emulate. This might include elements of presentation, use of vocabulary and phrasing, and use of linguistic features such as metaphors and similes.
- You can appreciate the challenges that children face when asked to write. Perhaps you can recall times when the writing task you set was done poorly by many children because they either did not fully understand it or because it was too difficult. For example, a teacher who asked his class to write limericks, but did not try writing some himself first, found that children were struggling to find rhymes for some of the towns and cities they wanted to include, such as Norwich, Coventry and Northampton.
- You can tailor writing to the needs and interests of your class when writing. This might range from including children as characters in your stories to including some of the words they are currently learning to spell, to focusing a story or piece of non-fiction writing on a topic many of them are interested in. A description of a Lionel Messi goal, or even of a pet, can fire children's imaginations and encourage them to write their own pieces.
- You can involve children in your stories, not only by making them characters, but also by giving them dialogue to read when the story is 'performed' or asking them to write and then read out the next section.
- You can target children's interests and even include them in a story. Children's self-esteem can be raised when they are cast as heroes in stories. When stories are read aloud, the children who feature can be asked to read their dialogue.
- You can elicit feedback from children and show that you respect and respond to it. This provides a model of how real writers write.
- You can develop vocabulary in a meaningful way by placing words children are learning into context.
- Sharing your writing with children gives you the opportunity to see how an audience responds to writing and helps you to appreciate the features of writing which engage and interest children.

- Your writing provides a model for children's writing and can be used as excerpts to explain how to write in different ways.

Despite the clear benefits of teachers writing for children described above, there are some barriers to this happening.

FOCUS ON RESEARCH

Ings (2009) reported the findings of *Writing is Primary*, a 15-month long action research programme, funded by the Esmée Fairbairn Foundation, and conducted in 2007/8. The researchers found 'overwhelming evidence that teacher confidence – or rather the lack of it – is one of the main barriers to progress [in writing]'. They found:

- modelling is more often undertaken through use of a text that has been prepared ahead of the lesson. Children do not often see adults writing in school; adults do not write at the same time as children.
- pupils do witness teachers writing but not in a creative context; it will be either a teacher completing a task at their desk or within the classroom alongside the pupils working on their own task, which may be different.
- teacher confidence should lead to pupil confidence in writing [but there is] little evidence that teachers see themselves as writers – writing tends only to be for professional purposes.

Ibid.: 22

In this chapter, we will look at ways in which teachers might be given greater confidence about their writing, as well as strategies and ideas for writing. We will identify different ways in which they can write for children and will show, through classroom examples, how these can work in practice.

Different forms of writing for children

Writing to children

This kind of writing can be used to create communication between teachers and pupils. The example in a case study later in this chapter involves a new teacher writing individual letters to her new class in which she tells a little about herself and asks the children questions about themselves. Such writing demonstrates that teachers value writing as a means of communication and can make writing meaningful for their pupils. Other possibilities could include tailored feedback on children's writing which poses questions and asks for more information, perhaps about a character in a story or a historical figure.

Modelling writing for and with children: shared writing

Many teachers are apprehensive about shared writing and admit to being afraid of making mistakes when acting as a scribe for children's ideas, or when creating their own text while thinking aloud. However, shared writing can be a very powerful tool, in that it demonstrates the writing process and shows how writers think, draft, edit and revise. Everyone makes mistakes when writing and these can be used effectively to engage children's interest and keep them alert to what is being written. Many teachers make deliberate errors when modelling writing and children enjoy spotting and correcting these. Usually, they will know that the teacher's mistakes are deliberate, but for the teacher the children's assumptions can be helpful when mistakes are accidental too!

Writing when children write

If teachers always took part in the tasks they set children they would have no time to make teaching points, give feedback or manage their classes. However, by occasionally writing for a short time when children are asked to write, they can show that they value the writing activity. Children tend to be very interested in what the teacher has written and eager to discuss it and make suggestions. This provides a model for them, as well as giving the teacher the opportunity to comment on the conditions she needs to be able to write successfully, including, perhaps, a quiet and productive classroom with no distractions.

Writing to engage and entertain children

This kind of writing can be done outside school and then brought in to share with children. Children enjoy having a story which is actually written for them and which might include some of them as characters. If a story is written as a serial, chapters can be read to and with children, who can then make suggestions for what might happen next, as well as writing their predictions and their own versions. Excerpts can be used for shared reading and the teacher can include some of the language features which are the current focus in English lessons.

What could you write?

Your decision on what to write for children will probably be determined by the nature of the texts which your class is currently exploring. You could write a complete text or you may wish to provide an example of a particular aspect of that genre. For narrative writing, these might include:

- story openings
- descriptions of settings
- descriptions of characters
- dialogue
- descriptions of dramatic events.

Find published examples before you begin to write and consider why they are successful and what features they include. If your focus was on settings, you might copy extracts from published children's stories and display these. They can then be used as a focus for discussion, and the display could be added to as children find their own examples, both from published work and their own writing.

For non-narrative genres, you might try writing short, formulaic poems, including haiku, cinquains, limericks, tankas and triolets. By writing these yourself, you will develop an appreciation of the challenges children will face when they write.

You may also write non-fiction texts, including prose, instructions and diagrams. A key benefit of working in this way is that you provide examples of what children are being asked to do: a sort of *Blue Peter* approach in which the prelude to an explanation of any craft project was to say, 'I've got one here I did earlier'.

By writing for children, we can create opportunities for what Dombey (2009: 10) refers to as:

a rich environment of meaning-making, where children are helped to draw on their developing understanding of a text to aid in the identification of its words, and to look at those words in close detail to refine their comprehension and avoid misinterpretation.

The case study below shows how a teacher used text, discussion and drama to create such an environment.

CASE STUDY

SHARING A STORY OPENING

David wrote a story which he wanted to share with a Year 5 class who were working on reading and writing story openings. He wanted to emphasise the importance of 'starting with a bang' (in this case literally!) so that the reader becomes immediately engaged and wants to read on. Before showing and reading the story opening, David explained that his idea was based on a true story of a friend whose parents' house had been visited by thieves in the night. He promised to tell them more later, but didn't want to give too much away about the story before he read it to them.

Before reading, David gave out individual word cards with characters' names and vocabulary which appears in the story opening. He read the words out and asked who had which, and told the children that after he had read the opening, he would be asking people if their words had been mentioned and, if so, in what context and what they thought the words meant.

car crash	ushered	Dad
larder	roof	Lodge
investigate	curtains	lead
gloom	Luke Foster	Jack Foster
wrist	dream	light switch
frantically	mobile phone	Army
danger	crept	999
stealing	squealed	grabbed
anxiously	almighty	furniture

THINGS THAT GO BUMP IN THE NIGHT

The car crashed with a crunch of metal and an almighty thud. Was he alive? Jack frantically felt his arms and legs. They seemed all right. He was all right, wasn't he? But his dad had his arm around his shoulders and was shaking him; not roughly, but gently, and he was speaking in a calm yet urgent whisper.

'Sorry, son, I had to wake you. I think there's someone on the roof. I'm going to investigate and I need you to keep quiet and not let whoever it is see you.'

Jack rubbed his sleepy eyes. 'There was a car crash, Dad. I was in it. There was a huge bang.'

'You were dreaming, Jack. The crash must have been the noise that woke me up too. I think there's someone stealing the lead off the roof. It sounds like they were throwing stuff off it.' Luke Foster passed his son a dressing gown and put an arm around his shoulders as he ushered him out of the bedroom and into the living room next door.

'Shall I put the light on, Dad?' Jack was about to reach for the switch when his father grabbed his wrist. 'Ow!' squealed Jack.

(Continued)

(Continued)

'Sorry, Jack, I had to stop you. If you put the light on, they'll know we're here and you could be in danger. Now listen, here's my mobile phone. You know how to use it. I'm going outside to see what's happening. It could just be animals, but if it isn't we'll need to ring the police. I'll be straight back, but if I'm not just call 999 and tell them there's an emergency and give them the address of the Lodge. OK?'

Luke turned and moved towards the door, which opened straight into the garden. The curtains were drawn and the room was almost totally dark, so he moved carefully to avoid bumping into their few pieces of furniture. Even in the gloom, Jack could see his father was still limping slightly.

'Stay out of sight, Jack, and if anything happens hide in the larder and call the police.'

'Dad,' said Jack anxiously, 'be careful, won't you?'

'Course I will, son. Don't worry. I know how to look after myself. Twelve years in the Army taught me that.' And with that, he carefully and quietly unlocked the door and crept outside.

Waugh, 2018: 1–2

After reading, David posed the following questions, asking the children to discuss each of them in pairs or small groups:

- *Why did Jack think he had been in a car crash?*
- *What do you think had actually happened?*
- *What do you know about Luke?*
- *Has your word been mentioned and, if so, in what context?*
- *Can you sum up the story so far in six words? – they don't have to be in sentence form.*
- *Do you think this is a successful story opening? If so, why?*
- *If not, how could it be improved?*

After spending around 15 minutes on the questions, the children were asked to listen to the story opening again and join in with reading, but this time with the dialogue spoken by the children who had the cards with Luke and Jack's names on them. They were encouraged to say their lines in an appropriately dramatic way.

Children were then asked to continue the story, initially by discussing and improvising it dramatically, and then by writing it in pairs after making notes and planning. David emphasised that he had planned the story before writing it and had also talked to his friend about the roof theft at his parents' house.

ACTIVITY

Consider how you would use the story opening above, or one which you wrote yourself, as a starting point for a series of lessons. Think, in particular, about the qualities of a good story opening.

If you attempt these lessons, prepare by finding examples of story openings from children's literature and displaying these in the classroom with accompanying questions inviting children's comments.

VOCABULARY DEVELOPMENT

In the case study above, there was an emphasis on vocabulary and the meanings of words. The National Reading Panel (2000) in the USA summed up research on vocabulary development by citing nine implications for reading instruction:

1. Vocabulary should be taught both directly and indirectly.
2. Repetition and multiple exposures to vocabulary items are important.
3. Learning in rich contexts is valuable for vocabulary learning.
4. Vocabulary tasks should be restructured when necessary.
5. Vocabulary learning should entail active engagement in learning tasks.
6. Computer technology can be used to help teach vocabulary.
7. Vocabulary can be acquired through incidental learning.
8. How vocabulary is assessed and evaluated can have differential effects on instruction.
9. Dependence on a single vocabulary instruction method will not result in optimal learning.

Ibid.: 4–27

Fisher and Blachnowicz (2005) recommended:

- ensuring the learning environment is **word rich**;
- addressing vocabulary learning as a **distinct area** in the curriculum;
- **careful selection** of appropriate words for planned teaching and reinforcement (for example, words that have parts found in many other words, such as medicine/medical/medicate).

Curriculum link

In the English National Curriculum (DfE, 2013: 15), vocabulary is identified in the 'Writing Purposes of Study': *'Effective composition … requires … an increasingly wide knowledge of vocabulary'*. Vocabulary also appears in the 'Spelling, Vocabulary, Grammar, Punctuation' section, which states:

> *Opportunities for teachers to enhance pupils' vocabulary arise naturally from their reading and writing. As vocabulary increases, teachers should show pupils how to understand relationships between words, how to understand nuances in meaning and how to develop their understanding of, and ability to use, figurative language. They should also teach pupils how to work out and clarify the meanings of unknown words and words with more than one meaning.*

> Ibid.

Synonyms

The National Curriculum states that in Year 6 children should learn: *The difference between vocabulary typical of informal speech and vocabulary appropriate for formal speech and writing (e.g. said versus reported, alleged, or claimed in formal speech or writing)* (DfE, 2013: 78). Among the terminology they should recognise and use is *synonyms*. By writing for children, you can extend their knowledge of synonyms and show how you try to vary the vocabulary you use.

CASE STUDY

DIALOGUE

Shannon wanted to work on writing dialogue with her Year 4 class. In their own writing and reading, some missed out or ignored punctuation, and written dialogue was sometimes rather stilted and dull. She decided that she would write a story opening which relied heavily on dialogue and would use this as a starting point for her class to work in small groups to write their own dialogue for different scenarios. Rather than simply writing dialogue for imaginary conversations, Shannon decided that she needed to consider carefully how children actually spoke, and how they thought that adults spoke, so she prepared herself, and the children, by introducing drama activities for pairs and small groups.

Shannon gave each group a slip of paper with a scenario written on it. She chose three different scenarios and ensured that each was worked on by at least two different groups. The scenarios were:

- *You arrive home from school late and your family have been worrying.*
- *You and your friends are playing in the park when you discover a bag full of money.*
- *A new boy joins your class and you want to make him feel welcome, but he is very shy.*

The children were asked to take on roles and have conversations. After around 15 minutes, Shannon asked each group to perform a part of their conversation for the rest of the class. She noted phrases the child characters used and the way in which the children spoke when they were in role as adults. She also wrote some excerpts on the board to show how they might be written down.

That night Shannon wrote a one-page piece of dialogue for each of the three scenarios above and created a presentation for shared reading. She practised reading the dialogue aloud and asked her partner if the language seemed appropriate for the characters, before making some tweaks.

The next day she read each of the dialogues to the children and then gave them roles and asked that they only read the actual dialogue and ignore all other text. She encouraged them to look at the verbs and adverbs which showed how the words were spoken and to use these to guide them on expression. She then asked the children how her dialogue could have been improved and what would have helped them to say their lines better.

Shannon's lesson illustrates the value of writing for children as a way of engaging them with grammatical and linguistic features of text. It also shows the importance of thinking carefully about how children and adults speak, and actually listening to children speaking in order to add verisimilitude to dialogue. Dialogue is a key element in much narrative writing and it provides a useful device for character development. Written well, dialogue can help the reader form opinions about characters and reflect upon and predict their actions. If phrasing and vocabulary is varied for different characters, there will be no need to identify the speaker for every line of dialogue. Where the speaker is identified, plot and character development can be helped by choosing verbs and adverbs carefully, so that an unpleasant character might *sneer sarcastically* while a nervous one might *stammer nervously*.

FOCUS ON RESEARCH

In order to identify approaches which have been found to be effective in the teaching of writing, the DfE (2012) drew upon research reviews of international evidence (What Works Clearinghouse, 2012; Gillespie and Graham, 2010; Andrews et al, 2009; Santangelo and

(Continued)

(Continued)

Olinghouse, 2009). In the section *Teach pupils the writing process*, the report states that we should:

- Teach pupils strategies/tools for the various components of the writing process such as: planning; drafting; sharing; evaluating; revising and editing; summarising; sentence combining
- Gradually shift responsibility from the teacher to the pupil so that they become independent writers
- Guide pupils to choose and use suitable writing strategies
- Encourage pupils to be flexible when using the different writing components
- Engage them in pre-writing activities where they can assess what they already know, research an unfamiliar topic, or arrange their ideas visually.

DfE, 2012:12

CASE STUDY

WRITING FOR AND TO CHILDREN

Bianca wanted to encourage her new Year 3 class to read and write for a purpose, while getting to know the children. Before the start of term, she wrote a letter which she adjusted slightly to personalise it for each child:

Dear ...

I am your new teacher and I am really looking forward to getting to know you. I'd like to tell you a little bit about myself and hope you will write back to me to tell me about yourself.

I come from Sunderland and went to primary and secondary school there. My favourite subject was English, but I also liked mathematics. What is your favourite subject?

At school I played in the netball and the football teams. My favourite football team is Sunderland. I still play football in a team, but we are not doing very well at the moment. We haven't won a match yet this season. Do you like sport? What do you like to play?

I have an older brother called Steven and a younger sister called Sophie. My Dad works at the Nissan factory and my Mum is a teacher. Would you like to tell me about your family?

My favourite television programme is Great British Bake Off. Do you like to watch television? Which programmes do you enjoy?

I do hope you will write back to me and answer some of my questions.

Best wishes

Miss Astori

When the children arrived in the classroom on the first day of term they each found an envelope with their name on it on their table, together with their pens and pencils and exercise books. Bianca had worked out a seating plan based on the comments of the children's Year 2 teacher and the envelopes enabled children to find their places quickly. Many expressed an interest in their envelopes and one asked if she could open it. Bianca said that as it was addressed to her she could certainly open it and so could everyone else.

The children read their letters and discussed them. Some children found some words difficult and Bianca explained that she would show everyone the letter on the whiteboard and read it with them before they wrote back to her. She talked with them about letters and how they should be set out, and told the children that they should try to answer the questions in their letters and that they could also add some of their own in their replies.

The letters proved a useful opening activity for the school year. Bianca found out more about her class so that she was able to talk with them about their hobbies etc., and she also discovered more about their writing abilities. In giving feedback to children, she was able to focus on content as well as transcription and she used the opportunity to write answers to some of their questions.

By writing to children, we create opportunities for developing understanding of texts as well as giving children starting points for their own, meaningful writing. We can also model the process and structure of writing in different genres.

FOCUS ON RESEARCH

Following a meta-analysis of research on writing, Higgins (2015) concluded that we need:

- explicit teaching of the *process* of writing and strategies which emphasise the different stages, such as planning, drafting and sharing ideas;

(Continued)

(Continued)

- emphasis on self-evaluation and developing pupils' capability to assess their own work through revising and editing;
- work on summarising texts in writing (such as through précis) and combining sentences;
- modelling of specific skills to support pupils, but where the support is deliberately faded out so that there is a gradual shift in responsibility from the teacher to the pupil so that they become independent writers;
- engaging pre-writing activities which help them to develop a range of strategies. This could be by helping them work out what they already know, or to research an unfamiliar topic, or arrange their ideas visually or thematically.

Tips for writing for children

Drafting and revising

If you lack confidence in your writing ability and are concerned that you might make mistakes when writing for children, try sharing your writing with a member of your family or a friend and be prepared to listen to constructive criticism. Doing this is not a sign of weakness: it's what real authors do. The authors of the book you are reading passed the chapters they had focused upon to each other and received, in return, text covered in tracked changes and comments. When we had submitted the book to the publisher, it was read by an editor who sent us comments and corrections to attend to. It was then typeset and proofs sent to us and a proofreader for further checking and the proofreader came back to us with queries. And even after such a lengthy process some typographical errors may have sneaked through! If you want to be a writer, you need to accept constructive criticism.

Read your work aloud to yourself

One of the first things you discover when you read your work aloud is that punctuation needs attention. If you have to re-read something to make it make the sense you intended, you probably need to look at your placement of full stops, commas etc. The next thing you may find is that you have repeated words or phrases. Try to read your work a few days after you wrote it, as if it was written by someone else. Be critical.

Seek feedback

Ask friends, colleagues or family members to read your work and accept their criticisms and suggestions are well meant.

Get some children to read it and give you feedback. Try doing this before presenting it to a whole class. In particular, ask about dialogue: *Would children actually say the words you have attributed to them? Are there words and phrases they might be more likely to use? Jack and the Roof Thieves*, an extract from which appears in one of the case studies in this chapter, was read to children in several schools before publication. Copies were given to schools and children wrote feedback and suggestions, many of which were taken on board.

Writing with readers in mind

Make your writing accessible to your readers, but don't be condescending. If what you write is full of vocabulary, idioms and phrasing which children won't be familiar with, they probably won't engage with it, but that doesn't mean that you cannot introduce them to new words and different ways of structuring sentences. The trick is to introduce these elements judiciously so that readers can work out meanings from context, which is just what adult readers do when reading in bed or somewhere where there is no dictionary available.

> If you are writing a story, ask yourself if your writing is likely to engage the reader immediately. Can you use the first sentence to draw the reader in and make her or him want to read on? Look at the two story openings below. Which would be more likely to make you want to read on and why?
>
> *Jo lived in a small house in a village near Newcastle with her mother and father and her younger sister, Anna. She has fair, curly hair and blue eyes and liked to wear jeans and tee shirts. Her mum worked in an office and her dad worked at a car factory. Jo had to share a room with Anna, because there were only two bedrooms in their little house.*
>
> or
>
> *It was on a dark and foggy March night, when Jessica was lying awake listening to Ellie's snoring, that her adventure began. Her legs hung over the edge of the bed, because her two sisters had taken up most of the room, and she was cold and uncomfortable. The bed was old-fashioned and had long legs which raised it nearly a metre off the floor. Jessica decided that she would wrap herself in the spare blanket and try to sleep under the bed – at least there would be more room! The springs creaked as she crept out of bed, but her sisters hardly stirred. As quietly as she could, Jessica slid under the bed and rolled herself up in a rather musty smelling blanket.*

In the first example, we find out about Jo and her family and where she lives. In the second, we find less information about Jessica's family, but there is already some action and the reader may begin to ask questions: *Why does Jessica share a bed with her sisters? Why does she decide to sleep under the bed? What might happen next?* The first example doesn't raise any questions: the reader waits to be told about events and may become bored in the process.

When we tell a story we need to give the reader information about characters and settings, but we can do this subtly by revealing things as the story unfolds. By gradually revealing information we can draw the reader into the story and encourage prediction, inference and deduction.

If you write a story, do you end sections with cliff-hangers?
Virtually every soap opera or drama serial ends with a cliff-hanger so that viewers will want to watch the next episode. By leaving your reader wanting more, you not only keep them engaged, but you also give them opportunities to speculate, predict, discuss and even write their own versions of the next section of the story.

Don't overdo adjectives and adverbs
We may encourage children to use lots so that they can rack up marks in tests, but writing can become tedious and unengaging if every verb has an accompanying adverb and every noun a series of adjectives. Make use of dialogue to develop characters. Use speech patterns and vocabulary to enable readers to identify characters without the need for repeated *she said, he said* etc.

Make use of illustrations
You don't have to do these yourself. You could download appropriate pictures from the internet. This can be especially helpful when you are describing an unfamiliar object or setting. They can also be a stimulus for children's own writing and can provoke discussion about descriptions and vocabulary.

Conclusion

Writing for children can be immensely rewarding for both teachers and pupils. There are few things more rewarding than reading your own story to children who are attentive and interested and can't wait to know what happens next. It shows that you value writing if you engage in it yourself, and it also helps you to understand the challenges children will face when they write. You don't have to have the skills of Michael Morpurgo or Anne Fine to write successfully: your enthusiasm and eagerness to develop your writing will help enormously, as will the feedback you receive from the children with whom you share your writing.

Further reading

The following texts provide ideas for creating a classroom in which writing is valued:

Bowkett, S. (2014) *A Creative Approach to Teaching Writing*. London: Bloomsbury.
Bushnell, A. and Waugh, D. (eds) (2017) *Inviting Writing Across the Curriculum*. London: Sage.
Chamberlain, L., with Kerrigan-Draper, E. (2016) *Inspiring Writing in Primary Schools*. London: Sage.
Daniel Hughes discusses the advantages of writing for children in:
Hughes, D. (2018) 'Sir, did you write this?', *Teach Primary* 12(2): 100–2.
Waugh, D., Neaum, S. and Bushnell, A. (eds) (2015) *Beyond Early Writing*. Northwich: Critical.

References

Blachnowicz, C. and Fisher, P. (2000) *Teaching Vocabulary in All Classrooms*. Columbus, OH: Merrill Prentice Hall.
DCSF (2008) *Teaching effective vocabulary: What can teachers do to increase the vocabulary of children who start education with a limited vocabulary?* Nottingham: DCSF.
DfE (2012) *What is the research evidence on writing?* Education Standards Research Team, Department for Education. London: DfE. Research report DFE-RR238.
DfE (2013) *The national curriculum in England: Key stages 1 and 2 framework document*. London: DfE.
Dombey, H. (2009) *ITE English: Readings for Discussion December*. http://citeseerx.ist.psu.edu/viewdoc/download?doi=10.1.1.430.2749&rep=rep1&type=pdf
Fisher, P. and Blachnowicz, C. (2005) Vocabulary instruction in a remedial setting. *Reading and Writing Quarterly 21*: 281–300.
Higgins, S. (2015) Research-based approaches to teaching writing, in Waugh, D., Bushnell, A. and Neaum, S. (eds), *Beyond Early Writing*. Northwich: Critical.
Ings, R. (2009) *Writing is Primary: Action Research on the Teaching of Writing in Primary Schools*. Esmée Fairburn Foundation. https://www.nawe.co.uk/Private/17646/Live/Writing-is-Primary.pdf
National Reading Panel (2000) *Teaching Children to Read: an evidence-based assessment of the scientific research literature on reading and its implications for reading instruction. Reports of subgroups*. NICHD.
Waugh, D. (2018) *Jack and the Roof Thieves*. Ludlow: YouCaxton.

5

WRITING WITH CHILDREN

KEY QUESTIONS

- What is the role of teachers and other adults in modelling writing?
- How can teachers and other adults write with children?
- How can examples of collaborative writing and strategies inform the way in which we write with children?

Introduction

In Chapter 1 on writing and spelling, punctuation and grammar, and again in Chapter 3 on scaffolding writing, we cited Vygotsky and his assertion that: 'What the child can do in cooperation today, he can do alone tomorrow' (Vygotsky, 1986: 188). This is known as the *zone of proximal development*: 'the distance between the actual development level as determined by independent problem solving and the level of potential development as determined through problem solving under adult guidance or in collaboration with more capable peers' (Vygotsky, 1978: 86).

In Chapter 4 we looked at the value of writing for children. In this chapter we will explore the potential of writing with children and explore how this can enable them to work at a higher level through adult guidance. We will examine three writing projects, one of which involved one to one work by a student teacher and a child, one which involved a whole class, while the other involved 45 children from 15 schools working with two teachers.

Creating resources for writing

Consider for a moment a piece of writing which you had to produce which was to be seen by someone else. What did you need to know before you began to write? It's quite likely that you will have written an academic essay recently in which case you probably needed to know some of the following:

- who would read the essay;
- how long it should be;
- what was an acceptable style, e.g. could you use the first person?
- what a good essay might look like;
- where you could find information to include in your essay;
- which form of referencing was acceptable;
- how it should be presented, e.g. line spacing, pagination, font size.'

There may have been tutorials to provide guidance and perhaps examples were placed online so that you could ensure that your work matched your tutors' expectations.

Now consider what children need if they are to be able to produce writing in different genres. Clearly, they will need you to model the genres and nurture their ability to write them with you and then independently, but you can back this up by creating resources for them to explore. These might include collections and displays of:

- favourite story openings;
- great descriptions of characters and settings;
- descriptions of exciting events;
- examples of interesting dialogue;
- unusual presentation;
- interesting vocabulary and phrasing.

Old books which are shedding pages can be saved from the waste bin and dissected to create displays so that children have ready access to examples. All of these resources help to create an environment in which literacy is valued, and a climate in which it is possible for children to write independently and with their teacher.

Why write with children?

An opportunity for everyone to contribute

How often do we comment that a certain child has wonderful ideas and makes a good oral contribution, but fails to match this with the quality of his or her written work? For some children this is due to specific learning difficulties such as dyslexia, while for others writing is a laborious process, perhaps due to difficulties with handwriting or spelling, punctuation and grammar. By writing with children, we can make use of their verbal contributions and sometimes confine their writing to brief notes of ideas and suggestions for phrasing and vocabulary. For example, a short story could be constructed, with children having mini whiteboards and working on these in pairs, and the teacher drawing ideas as the story unfolds and making use of the children's suggestions as he or she writes on a whiteboard or smartboard. Text can be edited and revised and re-read and children can be invited to look at individual sentences or descriptions or dialogue and work in pairs to offer alternatives and improvements.

Conducted well, such writing sessions can engage children's interest and provide them with material to continue stories and write their own endings. The whole-class elements of the story can be a source for spellings and vocabulary and a reference point for characters, plot and settings. Writing can be developed so that ultimately it is 'published'. Publication might range from being displayed on a wall, to appearing on the school's website or a rolling television display in the school entrance. It could involve printing and copying to disseminate more widely, including sharing with other classes and providing copies for parents and carers. It could even lead to actual publication for the wider public, as was the case with *The Wishroom* (Waugh et al., 2017) in the case study later in this chapter. There are clear benefits from working in this way.

Children can see how a publication is constructed

The process of writing from planning to publication can be modelled by the teacher, with children involved at every stage. This might occur within a lesson or over a series of lessons. In the case study below, a novel was written over several weeks and children were involved not only in writing, but also in proof-reading, editing and revising.

Writing provides reading material

By working with children to produce writing of publishable quality, we can provide reading material which they can relate to and take pride in.

The process encourages children to look at other texts for inspiration, ideas and presentation

In setting up a shared piece of writing, we can encourage children to look at other texts from the same genre so that they can examine presentation, types of vocabulary use and styles of writing. This enables them to consider and discuss texts for a purpose and presents opportunities for discussions, as well as providing children with ideas.

It enables children to broaden their vocabularies

By working with children, teachers can introduce them to words and phrases that may be unfamiliar to them, which they can understand because they are taught in context.

It enables children to produce something which might normally be beyond their capabilities

The end product of a shared writing project can be presented professionally, using desktop publishing techniques, so that children can have copies to keep and the work may be included in a class library, as well as on a school website. This celebration of writing can encourage children to want to produce further texts independently.

FOCUS ON RESEARCH

Writing can be thought of as a process made up of seven components. Pupils should be taught each of these components and underlying strategies. A strategy is a series of actions that writers use to achieve their goals and may support one or more components

(Continued)

(Continued)

of the writing process. Strategies should be carefully modelled and practised. Over time, pupils should take increasing responsibility for selecting and using strategies:

- planning
- drafting
- sharing
- evaluating
- revising
- editing
- publishing.

Writing strategies should be explicitly taught using the 'gradual release of responsibility' model. This can be repeated for each strategy. However, pupils will inevitably learn the strategies at different rates so it is important to recognise that the model is not a linear process. For example, based on observations of pupils' guided practice it may be beneficial to provide repeated modelling emphasising different aspects of the strategy. Teachers should introduce each strategy by describing how and when to use it. Then strategies should be modelled. Shared writing allows teachers to 'think-aloud' and share their thought process for each strategy with pupils. For example, teachers can model the revising process by posing questions to themselves:

- How could this be improved?
- Is some of the vocabulary and phrasing repetitive?
- Which synonyms could be used?

EEF, 2017: 9

This approach is illustrated in the case study below, in which a trainee teacher works closely with a pupil to enable the child to produce work at a higher level than he might have achieved working independently.

CASE STUDY

FOOTBALL REPORTS

As part of their PGCE Primary course, students at Durham University have some lectures in schools and follow these by working with children. Tom worked with a boy called Finley who was initially unenthusiastic about writing. During a reading assessment session, Tom had discovered that Finley was an avid football fan who regularly read magazines and sports sections of newspapers, focusing in particular upon his favourite team, Liverpool. For the following session, students and children were asked to agree upon topics which they would like to write about. Each would bring along some texts to provide background information which could be discussed and drawn upon. Tom discovered that the BBC Radio 4 programme *Word of Mouth*, hosted by children's author Michael Rosen, had recently featured an item on words and phrases associated with football. Tom drew upon this, an accompanying article (Hurrey, 2017) and various newspapers and websites to compile a collection of phrases, including:

Denied by the woodwork

Ghosting in at the back post

Almighty goalmouth scramble

Tense atmosphere

Schoolboy errors

Chorus of boos

Cancelled each other out

Whipped in a cross

Midfield battle

Cynical foul

Won a penalty

The atmosphere was electric

Taking it one game at a time

String of saves

Scored a hat-trick

A hatful of chances

A flurry of yellow cards

Brandished a yellow card

Back of the net

Must-win game

(Continued)

(Continued)

Game of two halves

Absolute screamer

Relegation dogfight

Glut of goals

Array of talent.

Tom and Finley discussed the phrases and how they tend to be used. Finley recognised many from newspapers and commentaries and was keen to apply them to a match he had recently watched between Liverpool and Everton. Together they planned a report on the match, which Finley wrote with support from Tom, who then took it away, typed it and imported pictures using a newspaper format. He brought the finished report to the school the following week and Finley was thrilled that his writing looked so professional and attractive. It was displayed in the school and Tom provided an extra copy for Finley to take home.

The case study illustrates the value of tapping into children's interests to inspire writing, as well as of good preparation and meaningful discussion. The quality of Finley's report was higher than he could have produced independently, but in writing it with Tom he recognised that his ideas could be developed through discussion and revised and edited to produce something he could be proud of.

Figure 5.1 Finley's football report

WRITING ALONGSIDE PUPILS

Ings' (2009) research revealed the value of teachers writing alongside pupils. His conclusions are exemplified with quotes from participating teachers:

> Several schools reported an increase in the number of staff who now regularly write alongside their pupils; in one school the number rose from two in November to ten by the following June. When teachers write in class, whether alongside learners or not, children begin to understand what goes into the writing process and the kind of strategies writers use to make meaning. The teacher appears to be an aspiring writer at that moment, rather than someone with all the answers at their fingertips.

> *As I write and rewrite, I change and debate things with myself and that's confusing and messy – more messy than I realised.*

> Having acquired a greater understanding of themselves as writers, of the complexity of the writing process and of the skills involved in teaching children to be reflective, teachers could see this already having an effect on their reading of pupils' writing:

> *I look at children's work, looking at far more than I used to and considering far more factors. The children are now aware that they can be critical readers, even if they are only at the early stages.*

Ibid.: 37

In the case study below, Shaun, a PGCE student on final placement, describes and reflects upon his experience of an initiative designed to improve children's writing, which involves teacher modelling.

A WRITING CYCLE

My school developed a new writing cycle, alongside a new marking policy, which has been interesting from a teaching point of view. The cycle is designed to produce higher-quality work from all pupils. The steps of the cycle are as follows:

1. The children are exposed to a particular writing style, i.e. persuasive, diary entry, discussion, retell etc.

(Continued)

(Continued)

2. After this, the teacher models how to design a plan for the writing as part of the teacher input, then children go and independently create their own, e.g. in a discussion text the introduction part of the plan is modelled – the children then design their own. This is repeated to produce arguments for, then arguments against and, finally, the conclusion – this can take multiple lessons.

3. Once the plan is complete, the teacher then begins a modelled write of the introduction – same topic – with deliberate mistakes that the children must identify and improve. The children will then write their own piece in the lesson – using the teacher's example as guidance.

4. The teacher then marks the work; however, no pen is used in books at this stage. Instead of writing in books, the teacher will use an assessment for learning sheet to record common mistakes children are making (this is one A4 piece of paper used to make notes on the whole class) and the common areas for improvement are then noted, e.g. misuse of their/there/they're or using parenthesis. The reason no pen is used to specifically identify areas for improvement in their books is because the writing cycle aims to give the child ownership over their work, and give them an opportunity to identify improvements independently, first.

5. The most commonly identified areas for improvement on the assessment for learning sheet then become the SPaG starter for the next lesson. All other areas identified are relayed to the class verbally at the start of the lesson; some children will receive individual verbal feedback if major improvement is needed or may even have one to one time with the teacher, e.g. a Year 5 child using none of the age-related writing features which are expected of them.

6. After the SPaG starter and verbal feedback, the children then have an opportunity to improve their writing independently – using the same-coloured pen.

7. After this lesson, all children's work is marked using the school marking policy. The teacher will identify areas for improvement bespoke to each child, using a green pen for comments.

8. In the next lesson, a common SPaG area for improvement is identified and is taught at the start. The children will then read their individual feedback and are given time to make suggested improvements – using a different-coloured pen to show this was a response to their feedback.

9. Steps 3 to 9 are then repeated until all sections or paragraphs are completed in the writing.

10. The finished piece then forms their 'polished piece', which is written up neatly into a separate book, which, over the course of the year, collates the children's best work.

11. After a lesson of taking pride in their work and writing it up neatly, the children are then given a *hot task*. This is where they use the knowledge gained over the two weeks or so, and write another piece of the same genre independently.

12. This work is then marked, but the child will make no improvements, as this is evidence of their progress and ability to write at age-related standard completely independently.

In my brief experience of the cycle so far, I support the idea that the children are exposed and guided so closely throughout the process. It is also great how their SPaG is monitored throughout and teaching is tailored to the class's needs. However, I feel it supports the children who are most likely to struggle more (to produce higher-quality writing) and may potentially hold back those children who are already writing at an age-related standard, as the children move through the stages together. I have found in lessons, when some children are still editing and making improvements, those who find writing easier in the class are becoming impatient as they want to move on to the next section. Usually, I allow these children to use whiteboards to start drafting their next section, but they do not write in their books until the teacher has shown a modelled write on whiteboard – essentially following step 3 on the writing cycle above. Also, it can take three weeks to produce a finished piece of work, which arguably discourages creativity and a passion and love for writing. The class I have been working with has wide range of children, some working at Year 3 age-related level for writing in a Year 5 class, with others moving on to writing at a Year 6 level.

The case study illustrates some of the benefits of a highly structured writing process in which teachers play a role which includes modelling writing. However, Shaun's reflections on the writing cycle indicate that such an approach may not benefit all children. It also raises questions about some practicalities which need to be considered when writing with children.

Some practicalities

There is no one correct way to write with children, but there are some aspects which need to be given careful consideration when we undertake such projects.

Where do the ideas come from?

Wright (2003:12) maintains: 'It's difficult for anyone to invent a story suddenly without being in a story-making frame of mind.' It is the job of the teacher in joint writing projects to initiate the writing, perhaps using a stimulus such as a story, picture or object or a piece of his or her own writing. It may be that a topic can be chosen and children can be asked to work in pairs or small groups to note ideas for a story opening before sharing these with the class. It is important to prepare for a lesson by having ideas in place, even if these are not used because the children take the writing in an unforeseen direction.

Who types the writing?

When children's contributions are handwritten and then collated into a story, ideally the class teacher will type the writing, correcting spellings and grammatical errors, but retaining the children's words and ideas. This gives an opportunity to look closely at children's writing and to assess their needs as well as their strengths. Typing can be time-consuming and teachers may wish to involve teaching assistants, but it is important that there is a consistent policy on error correction and that whoever types keeps notes on children's strengths and needs.

How much should we correct?

The end product should be a faithful reproduction of the children's words and ideas rather than a reinterpretation by the teacher. If children do not recognise the writing as their own, they will feel no ownership of or pride in it. However, if spelling mistakes and grammatical errors are left uncorrected, these may be reinforced and children may continue to produce them. By correcting without making major changes to the original, teachers have an opportunity to discuss spelling, punctuation and grammar. Where vocabulary is repetitious, it may be worth leaving this temporarily unchanged while inviting young authors to reflect on their writing and consider potential synonyms. This is often easier when writing is presented in typed form and changes can be made by children using a computer.

How do we keep a story on track?

If writing with children is to be meaningful to them, it is important that they have the licence to deviate from a storyline which you have prescribed. Simply asking them to fill in the gaps in your story structure will not give them any ownership of the tale and they are unlikely to see it as their own. However, if we offer carte blanche for children to take a story in different directions it may peter out as they (literally) lose the plot. A solution is to develop a framework for a story which enables children to write about the tale from their own perspectives and then discuss potential options for the next stage in light of different contributions. Where children wish to pursue their own storyline there is an opportunity to let them work independently or in pairs to write their own version which can then be compared with what the rest of the group produce.

All of the above points were considered when planning and developing a major writing project. In the case study below a structure was developed over a period of weeks and was adjusted in light of children's oral and written suggestions and contributions.

CASE STUDY

THE WISHROOM

East Durham Schools' 2016–17 Year of Writing involved schools coming together for conferences and a range of activities. One of these involved the author of this chapter, David

Waugh, supported by Sarah Myners, the deputy headteacher of the host school, writing a novel with a group of children from 15 schools.

Schools were invited to send two or three KS2 pupils to the host school on five occasions. The criteria for selecting them was left to the schools, but it was emphasised that children did not have to be high-ability writers and that teachers may wish to consider carefully which children might benefit most from the experience. Most children were in Year 6, with a few from Year 5 and one from Year 4. The authors included some very able writers and three, in particular, who were highly adept (and sometimes pedantic!) proof-readers. There were also at least two children who had been identified as dyslexic. On the first day we expected around 24 children, but in fact 40 turned up. During the course of writing the book some children dropped out due to illness and were replaced by others, and three children were invited to be additional illustrators so that the final, published novel, *The Wishroom* (Waugh et al., 2017), was written by 45 different children and David Waugh.

The opening of the story was written by David and printed copies, as well as a PowerPoint presentation, were provided at the first meeting. The scenario was that a large group of children from different schools had been chosen for a residential adventure week at Crampton Hall and they would need to get to know each other. Having set the scene, David and Sarah grouped the children into dormitories and asked them to chat and find out about each other. They were then asked to make notes and then write about meeting new friends at Crampton Hall. They went on to describe a sumptuous meal in the Hall's banqueting suite, where diners could choose any food they wanted and it would be served to them by a team of waiters and waitresses. An array of pictures was provided to stimulate ideas.

Writing was done in short bursts of quiet activity and was interspersed with discussion between children and as a whole group. They were asked for ideas about what might happen next in the story and were told that their writing would be taken away and typed and collated into two opening chapters. Each workshop began with a review of what had been written so far. Copies of the story were sent to schools so that children could read them in advance. This led to lots of discussion about typing errors and some feedback from children who wanted to make changes to what they had written. The text printed was shown in a PowerPoint presentation before children were introduced to the next stage of the story. For the workshop in which children visited the Wishroom, they were given these details the previous week so that they could think about ideas and prepare. The directions were:

WHAT IS YOUR WISH?

- Describe what happened
- How did you feel?
- How might it have changed you?

(Continued)

(Continued)

- Write in the first person
- You can wish for an experience, meeting someone etc.
- Describe what you see, feel, hear and how you feel
- Your wish will only come true while you are in the Wishroom
- After you leave, there will be no change to the world
- What will you agree to do in return for having your wish granted?

Before the workshop began we discussed briefly what each person's wish would be. These varied considerably, although three children wanted to meet Elvis Presley! One child, Evie, said she wanted to write about meeting her late grandmother, who had died months before Evie was born. We checked with her that her parents were happy for her to do this, especially as the book was to be published, and found that they were.

Children wrote enthusiastically about their wishes and were keen to share them with each other. Examples were read aloud and discussed and suggestions were made for improvements. Evie was reluctant to read aloud, but agreed that we could read her work for her. Children were transfixed by her moving account of a short meeting with her late grandmother. At the book launch a few months later, David asked if Evie would mind if he read her wish to the assembled parents, grandparents, teachers and children and she agreed. However, just before the presentation began, Evie said that she would be happy to read her work herself. More than 100 people were enraptured by her clear and well-delivered reading, with some being moved to tears.

The novel was written and illustrated in five workshops spread over three months. In the final session, the cover designer and illustrator, Stuart Trotter, guided children as they produced illustrations for the book. In April 2017, *The Wishroom* was published and officially launched in June at a banqueting suite in Peterlee, where those attending enjoyed afternoon tea and received free copies of the book, which was now available on Amazon both as a paperback and a Kindle version. Within 24 hours, three reviews appeared on the Amazon website, including, from one of the authors:

I think this is a brilliant book because I helped write it! You will be engrossed in this story. Enjoy! :-)

Why was the project successful?

The Education Endowment Foundation's meta-analysis of research (EEF, 2017) found that 'structured approaches with well-designed tasks lead to the greatest learning gains'. Writing *The Wishroom* involved considerable careful organisation and cooperation between schools and pupils. Each workshop was planned carefully, but allowance was made for children to take the emerging story in directions which were not necessarily those which we envisaged.

The children were given lots of opportunities to get to know each other and to talk about their ideas, as well as sharing different ways of expressing themselves. Their work was celebrated and shared throughout, both at workshops and between sessions via email. Throughout the project there was a clear expectation that the book would be published and that there would be an audience for it. Indeed, some schools use *The Wishroom* as a text for guided reading and as a stimulus for children's writing. The cover has every contributor's name on the front and inside and provides a lasting souvenir of the venture. At its peak, the book, which is available in paperback and as a Kindle version, reached 19691st position in Amazon's bestseller list of more than 6 million books.

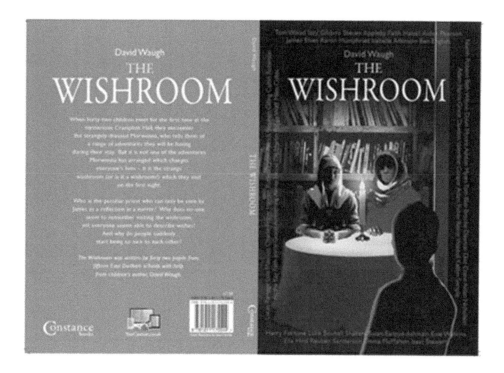

Figure 5.2   The cover of The Wishroom

A key factor in the success of the project was the presence and support of Sarah Myners, the deputy headteacher of the host school, who not only provided individual help for children, but also provided an important sounding board after each session as David reflected on how things had gone. When attempting joint writing projects with a class, you might consider how you might involve others, including the following:

- older children
- teaching assistants

- parents and volunteers
- colleagues.

In all cases, it is important that those who are supporting should know exactly what is required of them and what they need to consult you about. Helpers should be aware that they have a role in developing children's writing, but should not do the writing for them. Rather, they can discuss children's writing, provide suggestions and invite children to consider ways in which they might develop their writing. It is vital that helpers' efforts are valued and that they have opportunities to give you feedback, both on the children's progress and, where appropriate, on the way you planned and developed the lesson.

FOCUS ON RESEARCH

The Centre for Literacy in Primary Education (CLPE) examined its various projects and identified what they found worked well in writing in primary schools. One of the ten key elements identified was to develop an understanding of the craft of writing by engaging meaningfully with professional authors and their processes. The report maintained:

Having the opportunity to see and learn from a professional writer's practice is aspirational for children as writers and helps them to see the process of writing from a new and exciting perspective. Real life writers can bring a greater depth to learning about authentic writing processes. Teachers who engage with authors, and understand the editor's role are better able to appreciate the value of slowing writing down for children, allowing them time to plan and craft ideas, set the scene, create characters and formulate plotlines; revising and reviewing ideas along the way after response from others.

CLPE, 2017: 7

In the case study below Laura, a PGCE student on her final placement, describes how she and Christine, the class teacher, worked with children to develop a piece of non-fiction writing of a quality which the children might not be able to produce independently, but which they could achieve collectively and with support and guidance from their teachers.

CASE STUDY

YEAR 4 WRITING ABOUT WILDLIFE

During the summer term, pupils focused on an Explanation Text that was linked to their science topic – Living Things. In order to enhance pupils' writing, this was delivered over a two-week period that enabled time for outdoor learning, sensory discovery walks and key grammar skills which are linked to the text type. In order to engage pupils and to create a 'bigger picture' regarding what they would be writing about, pupils were asked to research different areas of wildlife such as ponds, animal and plant species, why we need bees and how we can protect wildlife. They then presented back to the class to share their expert knowledge.

Pupils also took part in an organised nature walk around the school grounds that included stops at the pond, forest area and fairy garden. At each stop, pupils were asked to write a variety of sentences which focused on sensory descriptions. As this piece of writing was delivered over a two-week period, pupils had time to plan, edit and improve their work. Planning and editing lessons focused on children creating well-crafted sentences that included key Year 4 objectives such as direct speech, plural possessive apostrophes and causal junctions. Originality was encouraged by asking pupils to research an interesting fact (about wildlife) to use in their writing. As a result of the above, children created a high standard of original and interesting writing.

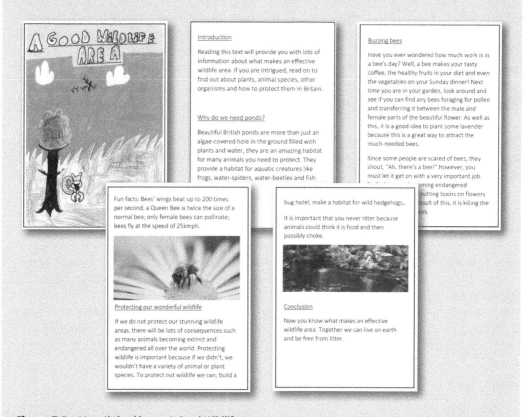

Figure 5.3   Year 4's booklet on A Good Wildlife Area

Challenges when writing with children

Identifying an audience

Before beginning a joint writing venture it is important to decide who might read the end result. This knowledge will determine how the text is written, the vocabulary and phrasing to be used, the subject and the presentation. Discussions with children about these features can be lively and stimulating and can foster an understanding of text types and their features.

Looking at examples of genres

In order to inform discussions about audience and presentation, it is important to provide examples of potential text types. Again, this can lead to discussions and investigations about use of language and presentation.

Identifying key vocabulary

Not only do teachers and children need to be aware of the kind of vocabulary appropriate for their writing, but they also need to consider how this can be varied using appropriate synonyms. An initial brainstorming session can provide a word bank which can be displayed and referred to, and can be a starting point for exploring synonyms using a thesaurus.

Discussion

Throughout the writing project regular discussions between groups and as a class will be needed so that everyone understands his or her role and what needs to be produced. Sometimes the writing might be by individuals and pairs, while at other times the teacher may act as a scribe for the children's ideas.

Sustaining momentum

Initial enthusiasm can quickly dissipate if plans are not made for new stimuli to help take the writing forward. This might come from the teacher writing a short piece to link what has already happened in a story to what might happen next, or it could be that pictures or film could be shown to stimulate ideas. In the case of *The Wishroom*, photographs of a range of attractive foods, pictures of shadowy stately homes and priest holes, and a timetable for a programme of events were introduced at the start of some sessions to promote enthusiasm and discussion.

Setting targets

If the writing is to be brought to fruition, targets need to be set so that children know there are deadlines to meet. Targets can also include using different language features and meeting learning outcomes, as well as doing research to inform the writing.

Conclusion

This chapter has identified ways in which writing with children can be productive and beneficial to children's writing development. In this final section, we sum up some key principles which should be taken into account when writing with children.

Key principles when writing with children

Giving children ownership

It is important that children feel that they have genuinely contributed to a piece of writing. We need to avoid taking it over or being over-prescriptive about the content and style, while still guiding them and making teaching points. This is a delicate balancing act. As teachers, we want to have an end product which will be admired by others, but if this includes language and ideas which the authors cannot relate to, children will take little pride in it.

Respecting children's ideas

Children sometimes want to take a story in a direction we had not anticipated or even wanted. On one occasion, the present author was role playing as a rather dodgy property developer in a story about a mysterious manor house, while the children played various roles, including as tradespeople. The project included both role play and writing a class story. At one point, a significant minority of the children decided they would like to kill my character off and there had to be a lengthy discussion before it was agreed that the character was necessary to sustain the plot. It was important not to simply dismiss the children's idea and to seek a compromise which the majority of children felt would take the story forward.

Reading and re-reading

Throughout a joint writing project, it is vital that the text produced is read and edited and revised in light of the authors' comments. If momentum is to be sustained everyone needs to see how the plot is developing and what their role is in moving it on.

Everyone can contribute

When teachers write with children there is an opportunity for every child to contribute in some way. This might be through oral suggestions, supported writing, illustrations, typing, proof-reading, editing, design or discussion. Even children who are not yet writers can contribute their ideas and work with a scribe to develop and record them.

The end product must be 'published'

Children need to see that their work is valued and can be presented attractively. As we saw earlier in the chapter, publishing does not necessarily mean printing, but may involve electronic presentation and distribution.

Emphasise the importance of planning and research

For *The Wishroom* children had to work in between workshops to devise their wish and to describe their role in one of the activities from the imaginary programme for their imaginary residential trip. For the work with children and trainee teachers in schools, both had to conduct research on the child's chosen topic in preparation for their next meeting when this would be drawn upon to produce an interesting piece of non-fiction text.

Invite published authors to talk to children

Teachers can model writing and scaffold it for children. They can work with them to guide, support and scribe and they can share their own writing with classes, but a visit from a published author adds another dimension to children's literary experience. Having an author show her or his work with a class, read extracts and discuss where ideas came from and how they were woven into a story can be fascinating and often inspires children to want to read and write. If an author can be persuaded to read and give feedback on a class writing project this can provide an incentive for children to produce good-quality work.

Remember the ZPD

This chapter began with a reference to Vygotsky's *zone of proximal development*, the concept that children can achieve more when working under the guidance of more experienced or competent peers and adults. Writing with children provides real opportunities to develop children's understanding of the writing process and to develop their skills with an end product in mind.

Further reading

To hear the episode of *Word of Mouth* with Michael Rosen which inspired the idea of writing a football report, see: http://www.bbc.co.uk/programmes/b095rrzx(accessed 4 July, 2018)

Hurrey, A. (2017) 15 of the most poetic phrases from the beautiful game. Available at:
http://www.bbc.co.uk/programmes/articles/5tcC9qRjZjcCD75C6G2KCLR/15-of-the-most-poetic-phrases-from-the-beautiful-game?intc_type=mixedcards&intc_location=radio4&intc_campaign=iplayerfooter&intc_linkname=article_footballmostpoeticphrases_contentcard23 (accessed 4 July 2018).

To find out more about research on writing, see:

DfE (2012) *What is the research evidence on writing?* Education Standards Research Team, Department for Education. London: DfE. Research report DFE-RR238.

References

CLPE (Centre for Literacy in Primary Education) (2017) *Writing in Primary Schools: What We Know Works*. London: CLPE.
EEF (Education Endowment Foundation) (2017). *Improving Literacy in Key Stage Two*. London: Education Endowment Foundation.
Ings, R. (2009) *Writing is Primary: Action Research on the Teaching of Writing in Primary Schools*. Esmée Fairburn Foundation. https://www.nawe.co.uk/Private/17646/Live/Writing-is-Primary.pdf

Vygotsky, L.S. (1978) *Mind in Society: The Development of Higher Psychological Processes*. Cambridge, MA: Harvard University Press.

Vygotsky, L.S. (1986) *Thought and Language* (trans., rev. and ed. A. Kozulin). Cambridge, MA: MIT Press.

Waugh, D., Sanderson, R., McMahon, E., Stewart, I., Kay, A., Joyce, F., Armstrong, G., Hood, A., Martin, E., Wood, T., Gibbins, I., Atkinson, I., English, B., Appleby, S., Halsall, F., Pearson, A., Harris, A., Dawson, G., Fisher, A., Waistell, R., Semple, K., Hird, E., Fortune, H., Boxall, L., Swan-Learoyd-Ashmain, S., Watkins, E., Ramage, L. Mawson, L., Frater, C., Rutter-Bryson, H., Gilling, P., Robinson, C., Elves, J., Humphries, A., Robson, N., Wilson, B., Moore, D., Myers, A., Blair, T., Dawson, B., Crane, D., Nicholson, A., Cooper, V., Watt, P., Colles, M., Pierce, J., Piercy, H. and Taylor, G. (2017) *The Wishroom*. Bishop's Castle: Constance Books.

Wright, A. (2003) *Creating Stories with Children* (5th impression). Oxford: Oxford University Press.

6

WRITING NARRATIVE, CHARACTER AND SETTING

KEY QUESTIONS

- In what way can we ensure high-quality descriptions within narrative writing?
- What makes a good character description?
- What makes a good setting description?
- How can we reveal character and plot within narrative in a variety of ways?
- What resources work best to inspire writing of narrative and character?
- How can we teach writing narrative and character in new and inspiring ways?

Introduction

Organising narrative writing into descriptive paragraphs with dialogue and a range of punctuation may seem a daunting task for children. It may also seem a daunting task for teachers to develop these multiple skills for their pupils. However, as daunting as it may be, narrative writing can also be the most rewarding writing there is. Children can write in the past or the present, they can write in the first or third person, they can tell imaginary tales or retell experiences such as school visits. Being a narrator means that you control the writing. You can choose the path which leads the reader. You are the master in real or imaginary worlds.

This chapter will explore how we can guide children to become better narrators of whatever story they are telling. We will look at how to develop oral storytelling skills in order to make a positive impact upon children's written language. If children are able to orally retell a story confidently then they are more inclined to be able to write confidently too, as their work will be organised into a clear and chronological way. For example, if children are able to orally tell the story of a school trip to the beach, or to orally tell the story of the Viking raid on Holy Island in 793AD, or to orally retell *Little Red Riding Hood*, then when it comes to writing any of these narratives they will know the structure first. They can then focus on adding the descriptive detail to this structure afterwards. This chapter will look at how to add descriptive detail, especially when describing characters and settings.

Dialogue to reveal character

Characterisation is where authors do not reveal the personality of a character simply through physical descriptions, but rather through what they do and say. This makes fictional characters seem like real people and real people feel as if they are really known to the reader. One way we can teach children to do this is through dialogue. When characters talk to one another, it reveals something more of their personality. Actions can do this too, but dialogue can be a subtle yet effective way of revealing character.

One way to teach children how to use a mixture of description and dialogue is to use a DAD planner. DAD is an acronym for *Description, Action and Dialogue*. When planning to write a narrative story like a pirate adventure or a retelling such as of a residential trip, a DAD planner can help children to consider not just what the key events are, but also what speech might occur, or did occur, throughout the narrative.

Looking at images of characters and imagining what they might be saying is an effective way of practising including speech in any kind of narrative. These images could be of familiar characters from books and television or can simply be random images of any people. The characters might be deep in conversation with each other or might be observing an event that is taking place.

Another way of examining speech and dialogue is examined in the case study below.

CASE STUDY

YEAR 2 CLASS USING COLOUR-CODED SPEECH

Sam, a Year 2 teacher, had been working on using inverted commas. The children had completed activities such as adding the correct punctuation to a dialogue between two characters. They had also punctuated statements from individual characters. They knew the terms 'inverted commas', 'speech' and 'dialogue' and also knew the meanings for these terms.

Sam showed her class some examples of speech on the interactive whiteboard. The sentence, *'I can't believe this!' said Jessica's mum.* was displayed. This text was written in black. Sam asked the children how Jessica's mum was feeling when she said this. Some children thought that she was angry. Others thought that she was surprised; others that she was sad.

Sam then highlighted the text and changed the font colour from black to yellow. She asked the class how they thought she was feeling now. Some changed their minds and decided that Jessica's mum was now happy. Others thought she was feeling ill. Others kept their original choices. Sam changed the colour of the font from yellow to pink. Some children thought that she was now excited. Others thought that she was disappointed. Some still kept their original choices.

Sam then displayed the following sentences on the whiteboard:

'Where are you?' said Steve.

This was in the font colour red.

'What do you mean?' said Namir.

This was in the font colour purple.

'Why?' said Mia.

This was in the font colour green.

'Wait for me!' said Mohammed.

This was in the font colour orange.

'I did it!' said Emily.

This was in the font colour brown.

The children were then asked to describe to each other how the people felt when they said these sentences. The children shared their ideas with each other. The answers varied considerably.

Sam asked her class why they could not agree with one another. The children seemed to think that it was because of the colour of the text. Most agreed with this. Sam asked them what they meant and one child told her that red was an angry colour. Some disagreed. One child added that purple was happy. This led to a lively debate about what colours they associated with what emotion.

Sam then changed the coloured font on all of the displayed sentences. She made them all appear in black. When she asked if this made any difference, the children found that it made little difference. They could still not agree how each character was feeling. Sam asked them what would help and the children finally all agreed that it was the word 'said' that needed changing. Sam asked them for some suggestions. The children offered words such as 'shouted', 'laughed' and 'screamed'. Sam then showed the same sentences but with the word 'said' replaced by another word.

'Where are you?' cried Steve.

'What do you mean?' whispered Namir.

'Why?' sobbed Mia.

'Wait for me!' laughed Mohammed.

'I did it!' cheered Emily.

These sentences were then discussed, but some ambiguity remained. The children could not agree on how Steve was feeling. They said that 'cried' could be good or it could be bad.

Sam asked if they needed more detail and the children told her that they did. She asked the children to rewrite the sentences adding detail in any way they thought would help. The more able children wrote multiple sentences such as, *'Where are you?' cried Steve with huge tears in his eyes. They dripped to the floor and onto his shoes. He could not find his dog anywhere.*

The less able wrote sentences such as, *'Where are you?' cried Steve with a red face. He was angry.*

These sentences were shared and compared on the carpet.

The case study above shows how speech can be open to interpretation. It was an effective lesson for teaching children the importance of clear description for the reader's clarification. The lesson can also be used to lead to other descriptive opportunities as in the following activity.

ACTIVITY 1

Ask children if they know what an adverb is. Ask them not only to define the word but also to explain how it can be used to enhance speech. Make a list of adverbs and ask the children to define each one.

- Could the children select an adverb and match it with some speech? How can adverbs be expanded into more descriptive language? Can the children select adverbs that do not end in '–ly'?
- What other ways can adverbs be used within speech and dialogue? Can the adverbs be part of the text within inverted commas?
- How can the *Descriptosaurus* by Alison Wilcox (2017) be used to enhance descriptions? How can it be used to enhance descriptions within speech? Can the children select more adventurous adverbs from this resource? How will these be used?

CHILDREN'S MISCONCEPTIONS ABOUT ADVERBS'

The adverb which corresponds to the adjective *good* is *well*. So the sentences below are incorrect:

John played really good.

I'm doing good.

Children often use 'good' as an adverb when 'well' would be correct, although you will rarely hear anyone make the mistake of turning *good* into *goodly* as an adverb (goodly is a rather antiquated adjective – a goodly woman). One of the reasons for the misuse of good rather than well is US television and films, in which characters often respond to questions like *How are you?* with answers like *I'm doing good* or *I'm good, thanks*. Sports pundits also often say that a player has *done good* instead of *done well*. Of course, it would be correct to say 'I'm doing good' if you meant to say that you were bringing benefits to other people. And if you were profiting from this, you could be doing well by doing good!

The same process of using adjectives instead of adverbs is extending to other words as well in advertising slogans – *eat healthy, think clever, shop smart* – and the trend seems likely to continue, perhaps because the adjective is shorter and 'punchier'. It is important, though, for children to understand that they should not use this type of construction in formal writing.

Although many adverbs end with –*ly*, it is wrong to say that an adverb must end in –ly. There are many common adverbs without an –ly ending, such as tomorrow, yesterday, always, soon and almost. Try adding each of these words to the following sentence to see how they work: *Alex rode a horse.*

When we first introduce adverbs to children, we often tell them that adverbs tell us more about or modify verbs. This true, but remember that adverbs can also modify adjectives, other adverbs, pronouns and noun phrases. (see Waugh et al., 2014)

Figure 6.1

Fairy doors and fairy land descriptions

Fairy doors are widely available and range from the plain to the ornate. Traditionally they are used as garden ornaments, but placing one in the classroom can have a positive effect on the development of language and imagination. It is recommended that they are secured in a place that children cannot reach in order to avoid little fingers pulling the door free. A teacher-led narrative can follow on from the discovery of such a door, particularly if each day something new is found connected to the door. There can be Lego tools left behind by busy fairies who had forgotten to take them home. Letters from the fairies can be written on font size 3 and left beside a magnifying glass in the classroom. Trails of fairy dust can lead to flowers from the garden. Once the teacher begins this narrative, the children tend to take over making links between the classroom and fairy land in the most creative of ways. A cobweb in the corner can become a rope that the fairies have climbed. A leaf blown in through an open door becomes a hat that has fallen from a fairy's head.

Once a narrative has begun, the descriptions can follow: *What might it look like behind the door? How can we shrink ourselves to fit through the door? Why might the fairies need our help?*

The Mysteries of Harris Burdick by Chris Van Allsburg (2011) features an image of a door at the bottom of basement stairs. The title says 'Uninvited Guests', suggesting a more sinister kind of fairy door. The Houghton Mifflin Books website features a very brief animated version of the image on 'Uninvited Guests'. When played, a snuffling, snorting sound can be heard as the door slowly creaks open. The creatures that children could describe behind this door would be very different from the stereotypical fairy. Butterfly wings could be replaced with bat wings. Dainty featured faces with pointed, elf-like ears could be replaced with piercing, beady eyes and a drooling mouth. 'Uninvited Guests' gives the opportunity for a more sinister fairy land.

But, more often fairy land is a place of magic and wonder, as can be seen in the case study below.

CASE STUDY

RECEPTION CLASS DESCRIBING A VISIT TO FAIRY LAND

Mai had placed a small, wooden fairy door in her classroom before school had begun. It was located above her whiteboard and secured with Blu Tack. The children were having their register taken and had not noticed the door. Mai had shared the story of *The Elves and the Shoemaker* (Southgate and Lumley, 2015) with her class the day before. The children knew the story well. Mai asked her class to tell her all about the story from the day before. The children retold the story, but Mai had to remind them of the chronology.

She asked the children to show each other their shoes. They did and then she showed them her own. She then asked if they knew what most shoes were made from. After a few answers, the correct answer of leather was offered. Mai asked the children if they knew what leather was. None knew, so she told them that it was animal skin. This prompted a surprised response and the examination of footwear on the carpet followed by a discussion that was very animated.

Mai said that she had got some leather the night before and tried to make her own shoes. She said that it was very hard and that she could not do it. But to her surprise the next morning the leather had been turned into shoes. Mai produced a pair of pointy leather shoes from her bag. The children exclaimed that they were fairy shoes. Mai nodded and told her class that a small door was near the shoes in her house that morning. She wondered aloud if the children had ever seen a door like the one she described. A lot of the children retold their experiences from Christmas with *Elf on the Shelf*. Then a child noticed the door above the whiteboard. The excited class asked their teacher to try and open the door. She tried but could not open it. The class asked her to knock at the door. She did but nothing happened.

Mai asked the children what they thought was behind the door. The children all agreed that it was fairy land. Mai then asked if it was fairies or elves that had made her the shoes. This prompted a discussion about the difference between fairies and elves.

Mai then rolled out wallpaper backing paper over the floor of the classroom. She explained that they were all going to draw pictures of what it might look like behind the door and who might live there. The whole class gathered in two lines either side of the paper. They used pencils and colouring pencils to draw the scene. It featured fairies, elves and even Santa. There were mushroom houses, tiny tree homes and an elf workshop.

The class then went off for *choosing time* and Mai worked with small groups on their section of the picture to annotate the scene.

The case study above contained a long introduction with lots of questioning. The teacher continued using the elf shoes and the door for several more lessons. These lessons did not need the lengthy introduction that was initially used and went straight into the children's activities like the ones that follow.

ACTIVITY

Ask children to imagine what the fairy homes might look like. Ask them what materials they might be built from. Ask the children to sketch and label the fairy homes.

- Could the children go outside and build models of these fairy homes? Can they work in teams, with partners or alone?
- What materials could be provided? What materials can be found in the school grounds? What will make the structure stay upright?

(Continued)

(Continued)

- Can the fairy houses accommodate additional features such as chimneys, ladders or a garden? What other features could be developed?

Watch 'Idents – France Advert' from the Literacy Shed or YouTube. Ask the children if they think this is how animals behave in fairy land.

- What other animals live in fairy land? What can they do that they would not be able to do in our world?
- Do the plants behave in strange ways too? Are there walking trees and talking flowers? What else might there be?
- Could the children write a list of nouns and verbs to describe the plants and animals and what they do?

Oral storytelling of narrative ghost stories

There are ghost stories from ancient cultures. The Egyptians, Greeks, Romans and Vikings all told some form of ghost story. The Victorians created a tradition for telling ghost stories at Christmas. Victorian authors such as M.R. James, Arthur Conan Doyle and Charles Dickens all wrote superb examples of the Christmas ghost stories. These ancient tales and old stories are not horror, but rather are a supernatural, eerie encounter with the dead. They are spooky, but not horrific. They made the reader feel unsettled, but at the end the book was closed and everyone had a little scare, but that was all. This kind of ghost story can lead to some creative writing opportunities in the primary classroom. There are variations of course, but the stories all tend to follow a particular structure that we can use with children. They are usually in the first person, the past tense, follow a triadic structure of spooky events and end with a cliff-hanger or some other form of suspense. If we use this same structure with children, they can add their own twists in plot and detail in description once the story has been planned and orally told.

There are stories that are suitable and can be read aloud to children in order to give them a range of examples. Books like *The Barefoot Book of Giants, Ghosts and Goblins* (Matthews, 2008), *Usborne Illustrated Ghost Stories* (Various authors, 2015) or *The Orchard Book of Goblins, Ghouls and Ghosts* (Waddell, 2006) all contain some suitable stories. Older collections by Ruth Manning Sanders, Dinah Starkey and Kevin Crossley Holland have some timeless classics too.

There are animations that can support this genre of writing too: 'Alma', 'Dark Matters' or 'Francis' are good examples. These can be found on The Literacy Shed and on YouTube. Each shows spooky events such as doors opening by themselves, lights going out, objects moving by themselves, shadows lengthening or creepy music.

But the first step in creating a narrative ghost story is to choose the setting. Any setting will do as long as it is abandoned. If it is abandoned then it automatically becomes slightly unsettling. An abandoned beach, school, shop, hospital, forest or anywhere the children select themselves will be suitable. The first-person narrative then needs to provide a reason as to why the children would be alone in an abandoned setting. This is what sets apart spooky stories from spooky films: we get to understand the mind of the character. We can explain *why* they are there in that setting and not running home as fast as they can.

Some examples could be that they are there on a dare, to find something dropped earlier in the day such as a phone, to find a missing pet or relative, for an adventure to see if it really is as haunted as legend suggests, or even to film a YouTube video.

Then the children add three spooky events which they can use from the stories they have read or animations they have seen or from their own imaginations. It is at this point in the narrative that they meet a ghostly figure and leave their story on a cliff-hanger ending.

How they describe their ghostly figure is something explored in the case study below.

CASE STUDY

YEAR 6 CLASS

Sanchez, a Year 6 teacher, had been exploring portrait drawings in art lessons. He had photocopied the whole class's portraits, including his own. The class were also learning about writing ghost stories and had read most of *A Christmas Carol* by Charles Dickens. Sanchez had found a clip from the 2009 animated movie with Jim Carrey. He showed the children the scene where Scrooge returns home to see Marley's ghost in the door knocker from his front door. In it, the music becomes slow and eerie. The ghostly face is a glowing green and looks serene. Then the ghost screams and the face twists grotesquely. Even the children who had seen the film before jumped at the moment when Marley shouted 'Boo!'. There was much laughter and clutching of chests.

Sanchez went back to the moment where Marley's face changes and paused the film at exactly the moment where the teeth fly from the mouth and the ghost wears a look of utter rage. Sanchez then showed the class his own A4 photocopied portrait and told his class he was going to make his own face look scary like the one in the video clip. He added lines around the cheeks and eyes. He changed the shape of the eyebrows to make them angry and hairy. He then added wild hair and coloured the eyes all black. The effect was to make the class teacher look like an undead creature.

Sanchez then told his class that they were going to do the same to their own portrait or to a friend's portrait. The class enjoyed this activity enormously and added gaping eye sockets, exposed brains, lolling tongues and rotting flesh. Sanchez then asked the children to label the portrait with nouns, verbs and adjectives. These were then written into descriptive sentences and shared with each other.

The case study above was an introduction to describing ghostly portraits. The rest of the week was spent using the 'vandalised' portraits to add more description. There was a lesson on using figurative language such as personification, metaphor and simile. There was another on varied sentence length for effect. There was another on describing what they would feel if they were to meet this ghost. The children described feeling and emotions in their writing linked to physical action – for example, gasping for air, wringing of hands or eyes widening. The teacher knew that these activities were suitable for his Year 6 class, but they may not be suitable lower down the school.

ACTIVITY

Create ghostly portraits for your own class. Ask children to add descriptive language labels and figurative language phrases.

- What type of figurative language will you focus on? What resources can you use to support this activity?
- Are there short stories or animations that you can use to complement the ghost story narrative?

Think about how the children will tell their narrative stories.

- Will you use torches in a darkened classroom? Could you use the outdoors as a stimulus for their storytelling? How can technology be used to support telling ghost stories?
- Once the stories have been told, how can detail be added in writing? What other resources could be used to support this writing process?

Hyperbole to reveal character

Figurative language can be a difficult area of description for children. It is an abstract concept to describe something as being something that it is not. Lemony Snicket, in his book *The Bad Beginning* (2016) from the *Series of Unfortunate Events*, says:

It is very useful, when one is young, to learn the difference between 'literally' and 'figuratively'. If something happens literally, it actually happens; if something happens figuratively, it feels like it is happening. If you are literally jumping for joy, for instance, it means you are leaping in the air because you are very happy. If you are figuratively jumping for joy, it means you are so happy that you could jump for joy but are saving your energy for other matters.

Ibid.: 59

Hyperbole is a type of figurative language that children frequently hear, but they do not necessarily know what it is called. They hear their family using hyperbole like *'I've asked you to pick up your dirty washing a thousand times!'* or their friends might say *'I've just walked for miles and miles to get here!'* Children know that they are hearing exaggeration, but perhaps not that this is defined as hyperbole.

The website yourdictionary.com has many examples of hyperbole written specifically for children to help them to understand this form of description. It also shows examples of hyperbole used by authors and even used in television advertisements. Once children grasp the concept of how hyperbole is used all around them, they can begin to use it confidently in their writing, as can be seen in the following case study.

CASE STUDY

YEAR 3 WRITING VIKING BOASTING

Isla, a student teacher working on her final placement in Year 3, was discussing the topic of Vikings with her class. She asked them to review what they had learnt so far. She asked them what they had found interesting and then asked them what they wanted to find out next.

One of the children had asked her what the Vikings used to do to for pleasure. Isla told the class that they enjoyed swimming, wrestling, listening to saga stories and playing games such as *Hnefatafl*. She also told them that they had boasting competitions where a group of Vikings would gather in a *mead hall* and boast of great deeds they had performed in the past. She explained that these deeds would be greatly exaggerated and gave an example of killing a hundred dragons with a spoon or wrestling Thor and making him cry.

Isla then explained that this was called *hyperbole*. She asked the children to repeat the word, first to her, then to a talk partner and back to her again. She told the class that they were going to write their own Viking boasts using hyperbole. She showed several sentence starter examples on the whiteboard. These included:

I swam over . . . in less than . . .

I wrestled a . . . and made it . . .

I climbed . . . using only my . . .

I defeated a . . . with just a . . .

I jumped over . . . while juggling . . .

Isla then asked the children to write as many examples as they could in ten minutes. She supported the less able by giving them photocopied starter prompts like the ones on the board.

After the ten-minute activity was completed, the class gathered on the carpet. Isla showed the children an image of the actor Dwayne Johnson. Most of the class knew him

(Continued)

(Continued)

as *The Rock*. The image showed the actor screaming ferociously, the veins on his neck were popping and his biceps bulging. Isla explained that when the Vikings boasted they would speak like Dwayne Johnson appeared to be speaking in this image. She went on to explain that when the children shared their favourite boasts then they should deliver their lines in this way too. She said that she didn't want timid, expressionless hyperbole boasts; she wanted them delivered like a Viking.

The children enjoyed shouting their boasts to each other. Some volunteers then delivered their favourite sentences to the class.

The children enjoyed the drama-based literacy lesson. Their boasts included: *'I swam through a lava-filled volcano in my trunks!', 'I defeated an army of ogres by just blinking!'* and *'I'm so strong that when I break wind, it can blow away an entire army!'*

By revealing past deeds such as these we are revealing character. The writing in this case study was in the first person, but it is easily transferable to third-person writing as in the activity below.

ACTIVITY

Show the children the beginning of the animation *The Saga of Biorn* from YouTube or The Literacy Shed. It is about a Viking warrior on a quest to die in battle in order to get to Valhalla – Viking heaven. The opening line from the narrator is *'Who is this Viking and what made him throw a dwarf from a cliff?'*

- What other evil deeds could this Viking have done in his life? Can the children use hyperbole to describe each deed? Think carefully about matching the deeds to this character or one that you want to create.
- What else can reveal character other than past actions? What other animations or texts can be used to support character descriptions?

FOCUS ON RESEARCH

Hyperbole is a device that we employ in our day-to-day speech. For instance, when you meet a friend after a long time, you say, 'It's been ages since I last saw you.' You may not have met him for three or four hours, or a day, but the use of the word 'ages' exaggerates this statement to add emphasis to your wait. Therefore, a hyperbole is an unreal exaggeration to emphasise the real situation. Some other common hyperbole examples are given below.

- My grandmother is as old as the hills.
- Your suitcase weighs a ton!
- She is as heavy as an elephant!
- I am dying of shame.
- I am trying to solve a million issues these days.

In our daily conversation, we use hyperbole to create an amusing effect, or to emphasise our meaning. However, in literature it has very serious implications. By using hyperbole, a writer or a poet makes common human feelings remarkable and intense to such an extent that they do not remain ordinary. In literature, usage of hyperbole develops contrasts. When one thing is described with an over-statement, and the other thing is presented normally, a striking contrast is developed. This technique is employed to catch the reader's attention (see the Literary Devices website at https://literarydevices.net/hyperbole/).

Conclusion

Detailed character and setting descriptions can make narrative stories come alive for the reader. We can imagine stepping into Hogwarts and meeting Harry because of J.K. Rowling's use of language. We can picture standing side by side with Aslan facing the White Queen's horde because of C.S. Lewis's vivid imagery. These authors were not born good at writing. It is a skill that is developed through practice. By giving children the opportunity to write frequently, and by guiding them through writing processes in the way shown throughout this chapter, then we are also giving them the opportunity to become better storytellers. But not just storytellers who can retell a structure of a story: rather, storytellers using the written word who can paint pictures with their words.

Further reading

For ideas and guidance on narrative, character and setting, see:

Bowkett, S. (2014) *A Creative Approach to Teaching Writing*. London: Bloomsbury.
Chamberlain, L., with Kerrigan-Draper, E. (2016) *Inspiring Writing in Primary Schools*. London: Sage.

Recommended websites

Harris Burdick animated images –http://www.houghtonmifflinbooks.com/features/harrisburdick/inspired_by_burdick.html

Idents – France Advert – https://www.literacyshed.com/the-advert-shed.html

Ghost animations Alma and Francis – https://www.literacyshed.com/the-ghostly-shed.html

Ghost animation Dark Matters – https://www.youtube.com/watch?v=pBpu9sgw_gc

Marley ghost in door knocker scene from *A Christmas Carol* – https://www.youtube.com/watch?v=h3-oim446M8

Your Dictionary examples of hyperbole – http://examples.yourdictionary.com/examples-of-hyperbole-for-kids.html

Saga of Biorn animation – https://www.youtube.com/watch?v=MV5w262XvCU

References

Matthews, J. (2008) *The Barefoot Book of Giants, Ghosts and Goblins*. London: Barefoot Books.

Snicket, L. (2016) *The Bad Beginning*. London: Egmont.

Southgate, V. and Lumley, R. (2015) *The Elves and the Shoemaker*. London: Ladybird.

Van Allsburg, C. (2011) *The Mysteries of Harris Burdick*. London: Anderson Press.

Various authors (2015) *Usborne Illustrated Ghost Stories*. London: Usborne.

Waddell, M. (2006) *The Orchard Book of Goblins, Ghouls and Ghosts*. London: Orchard Books.

Waugh, D., Allott, K., Waugh, R., English, E. and Bulmer, E. (2014) *The Spelling, Punctuation and Grammar app*. Morecambe: Children Count (available through the App Store).

Wilcox, A. (2017) *Descriptosaurus*. Oxford: Routledge.

7

WRITING POETRY

TEACHERS' STANDARDS

This chapter will help you with the following Teachers' Standard:

3. Demonstrate good subject and curriculum knowledge
- have a secure knowledge of the relevant subject(s) and curriculum areas, foster and maintain pupils' interest in the subject, and address misunderstandings;
- demonstrate an understanding of and take responsibility for promoting high standards of literacy, articulacy and the correct use of standard English, whatever the teacher's specialist subject.

KEY QUESTIONS

- What types of poems should be used as models in the primary classroom?
- How should poetry be presented and analysed?
- What poetry might be used as inspiration for creative writing?
- Why is poetry important in primary classrooms?

Introduction

Poems are generally shorter than stories and as such can be shared much more readily in the classroom as a quick introduction to a lesson or to be read for pleasure. This is also the case when writing poetry. Some children find writing longer narratives difficult, as they have not developed their writing stamina.

Poetry is something which some teachers find difficult to teach. It can have an association in schools with rather dry recitation and language which can be difficult to understand. However, this chapter seeks to show how poetry can be taught in an inspiring, creative and, most importantly, enjoyable way. We will explore how to change descriptive techniques and play with language to make poetry exciting in the classroom. The links between the written and the spoken word are many and we will examine how performance poetry can lead to better drafting, editing and improving techniques.

Poems can be used to study language for effect, as every word has been carefully selected and placed in precisely the place the author has intended. Despite this careful word place-ment, poems are very interpretive. Each reader responds differently and interprets the language in their own way. Poems generally encourage the reader to think past the literal and move into the figurative. Poems can, therefore, be used as a device to help children describe things in a figurative or abstract way.

When children look at poems such as haikus or those written using iambic pentameter, they begin to see how language can be broken up into syllables. They can begin to see the rhythm of everyday language. They begin to hear patterns in language which we all use on a daily basis. Then, hopefully, we can help children to hear the beauty in all spoken word. Even when they talk to us, their families and each other there is a rhythm, a pattern and a change in pitch and tone. By studying poetry, we are studying and raising awareness of our language. This chapter will look at how language can be used, through poetry, to enhance our literary skills orally and in our written voice.

FOCUS ON RESEARCH

Hughes (2007: 1) analysed research on poetry and concluded:

- Poetry awakens our senses, helps us make connections to others, and leads us to think in synthesizing ways, as required by the use of metaphor.
- Paying attention to the language and rhythms of poetry helps build oral language skills.
- Children with well-developed oral language skills are more likely to have higher achievement in reading and writing.
- Creative applications of new media that build on the literacies students have already developed outside of school can help teachers tap into the literacy-enhancing power of poetry.

Hip hop and Shakespeare's sonnets

Lyrics from hip hop music and the poetry of Shakespeare share similarities in their structure and use of rhyme. Most of Shakespeare's sonnets are written in the rhyme scheme of iambic pentameter. This is a line which consists of ten syllables, for example, KaBOOM, KaBOOM, KaBOOM, KaBOOM, KaBOOM.

This can be seen in Sonnet 18:

Shall I / com PARE/ thee TO / a SUM / mer's DAY?
Thou ART / more LOVE / ly AND / more TEM / per ATE.

Most hip hop verses use iambic pentameter or something close to it.

In Eminem's 'Lose Yourself' the verse is not quite written in iambic pentameter, but it does follow a similar pattern, especially when listened to rather than being read. The lyrics are:

His PALMS are SWEATy, KNEES weak, ARMS are HEAVy
There's VOmit ON his SWEATer alREADy, mom's spaGHETTi
He's NERVous, but ON the SURFace he LOOKS calm and READy
To DROP BOMBS, but HE keeps ON forGETtin
What HE wrote DOWN, the WHOLE crowd GOES so LOUD
He OPens his MOUTH, BUT the WORDS won't come OUT
He's CHOKin, how EVeryBODy's JOKin NOW
The CLOCK'S run OUT, TIME'S up OVer, BLOah!

The verse is meant to be read like iambic pentameter of KaBOOM, KaBOOM, KaBOOM, KaBOOM, KaBOOM. It sounds like a heartbeat. When performing the lines, that is the rhythm that is meant to be maintained in both Shakespeare and in hip hop. Hip hop is all about performing the lyrics rather than reading them. This is also the case with Shakespeare's work. The words are meant to be spoken rather than read. His plays were written for actors to deliver the lines to audiences as an immersive experience.

When Shakespeare wanted to stress the importance of what his characters were saying to the audience, he wrote the lines in rhyme. For example, Hamlet says:

The time is out of joint, O cursed spite
That ever I was born to set it right!

The play *Othello* also follows this rhyming device when Iago says:

I thank you for this profit, and from hence
I'll love no friend, since love breeds such offence.

The rhyme can also be more of a half rhyme, something which hip hop artists also use frequently. For example, Grand Master Flash and the Furious Five wrote in 'The Message':

Rats in the front room, roaches in the back
Junkies in the alley with a baseball bat.

The hip hop artist, writer and historian Akala makes the point that iambic pentameter works like a mnemonic so as to make the lines easier to remember for the actors and for the audience.

The topics explored by Shakespeare are still topics which hip hop artists explore now. For example, compare Shakespeare's line from *As You Like It*, 'I came, saw and overcame' to Jay Z and Linkin Park's line from Numb/Encore, 'I came, I saw, I conquered.'

The topics Shakespeare frequently explored were murder, madness, revenge, greed and love, all of which hip hop artists explore in their lyrics too. Akala has set up the Hip Hop Shakespeare Company in London. He says that hip hop and Shakespeare share 'a unity in human culture, a unity in the ideas that humans pursue; and to inspire people towards their own form of artistic literary, cultural, and societal excellence' (Akala, 2011).

The Hip Hop Shakespeare Company is a music theatre production company aimed at exploring the social, cultural and linguistic parallels between the works of William Shakespeare and those of modern day hip hop artists. Akala and his team travel to places, including schools, to run creative writing and performance poetry sessions for children. The ideas they explore are that hip hop and Shakespeare deliver the same message: 'to transmit knowledge and question the world around us' (ibid.). There are links to Akala's lecture on hip hop and Shakespeare, including his rap version of Sonnet 18, at the end of this chapter.

However, Shakespeare does not have to be the only inspiration to help us to teach rhyme, as can be seen in the case study below.

CASE STUDY

YEAR 3 CLASS WRITING IN RHYME BASED ON KIRK HENDRY'S 'JUNK' ANIMATION

Rachel, a Year 3 teacher, asked her class to list rhyming words for *red, blue* and *green*. Several suggestions were made and she wrote these under each colour. She then asked the children what rhymed with *orange*. A few nonsense words were suggested, but nothing that was an actual real word. Rachel then asked them what rhymed with *purple* and got the same response. The word *silver* was next and this too proved difficult.

Rachel explained that in the English language there are some words that rhyme easily and others that have few or no rhymes. She then showed her class the animation 'Junk' by Kirk Hendry. It is about a boy who ate nothing but junk food and then moved on to eating actual junk as well, including cement, barbed wire and tar. The unfortunate boy ended up trying to eat an entire oil tanker's cargo whole and, sadly, died doing so. It is a cautionary fantasy reminiscent of Edward Lear's *Book of Nonsense*, Heinrich Hoffman's *Der Struwwelpeter* or even David Walliam's *World's Worst Children* books.

Rachel then told her class that they were going to make up their own version of 'Junk' but replace the character Jasper O'Leary with a different character, and replace the junk food with another food. This would be a shorter poem that still followed the same storyline; their character would meet an unfortunate end due to their obsession with a particular kind of food. The food that they chose should be a word that could easily rhyme with another word. She gave the examples of cheese, hot dog and bread. The children then worked in pairs to discuss what food they would choose. Rachel modelled the lines:

There once was a girl who ate nothing but cheese,
She gobbled it up with the greatest of ease.

and

There was a man who always ate hot dogs,
He kept them in a wooden pair of clogs.

and

There lived an old woman who only ate bread,
Some people said she was mad in the head.

The children had to choose their own food, but could use the sentence starters that Rachel used if they wanted to. The teacher explained that they would only write the first two lines then share these with each other. The class wrote the first two lines of the poem and read them to each other at their tables. Rachel worked with the lower-ability children, who discussed their ideas and then wrote together.

The class then gathered back onto the carpet to work in mixed-ability pairs. Rachel gave them the words *away*, *night* and *down*. The children had to write these words and words that rhymed with them. They were then asked to write the next six lines of their poem using the three pairs of rhyming words. She supported the less able by giving them sentence starters. The class then shared their eight-line poems on the carpet with each other.

Rhyming can be difficult for children. The class had spent several lessons prior to this lesson working on rhyming words. They knew that they came at the end of the line and knew that the spelling could be different as long as the sounds were the same. The teacher had given them the tools before the lesson to enable them to succeed in writing their own rhyming poems.

ACTIVITY 1   RHYMING COUPLETS

Read the children a picture book written in rhyming couplets such as *Giraffes Can't Dance* by Giles Andreae or *Moo, Baa, La La La* by Sandra Boynton. As you read it, stop before reading the rhyming word and ask the children what they think it will be. Consider:

- How could this be adapted for older children? Could song lyrics be used in this way? Can hip hop music be suitable for this kind of activity? Which songs will be suitable for you to use?
- What other picture books are there that are written in rhyming couplets? Which of these would be suitable for this activity?
- Are there any other animations narrated in rhyming couplets other than 'Junk'? How can these be used to teach rhyme?

Research has shown a correlation between children's sensitivity to rhyme and successful acquisition of reading skills. Bryant et al. (1990) investigated children's linguistic capabilities at age three and four, and later assessed their reading and spelling capabilities, aged six and seven. They found that children who developed an awareness of sounds and the poetry of language early were generally more successful in reading, writing and spelling. Goswami (1990), too, found that pre-reading rhyming skills were a strong indicator of future reading development and acquisition of key reading skills. It is important, therefore, that rhyme is used in conjunction with phonics to support reading development.

Whitehead (2007: 38) also maintained that phonological awareness can be developed in young children through their encounters with rhymes, asserting:

Many poor readers are remarkably insensitive to rhymes and to the beginning sounds of words, but very young children with an interest in the sounds and poetry of language may well be on the road to reading, writing and spelling successfully.

Saga and epic poetry

Saga poetry is often associated with Germanic and Icelandic writing. It is usually a narrative story such as *Sigurd the Dragon Slayer*, *Brynhild the Valkyrie* and the Viking chieftain *Ragnar Lothbrok* (made famous in the Amazon TV series *Vikings*).

Epic poetry is also usually a narrative centring on a hero and their adventures through a particular culture, historical time period or a list of heroic deeds. Examples of epic poetry are *The Odyssey*, *Beowulf* and *Gilgamesh*. *Paradise Lost* and *The Divine Comedy* are also epic poems. In their essence, they are stories: stories of adventure, usually focusing on a central character showing their flaws, such as pride or greed, as well as their more positive attributes, such as bravery or cunning. This central character usually goes on some sort of actual journey or a spiritual one. When they return they are changed, in most cases, for the better.

In the Babylonian epic poem of *Gilgamesh*, the central character is arrogant and selfish. He meets a hero named Enkidu who travels with and teaches Gilgamesh to become a wise and selfless leader.

Becoming a better monarch seems to be a common thread through epic poetry. In *Beowulf*, the central character allows his love of gold to affect his decision making throughout the narrative. It is only as he breathes his last, while looking at a golden hoard stolen from a dragon, that he realises the error of his ways.

Unlike epic poetry, saga poems tend to just tell the stories and leave out the theme of journey and return. They can, of course, involve a journey of some sort, but tend just to focus on the adventure or adventures that the central character has. It is more about the great deeds performed than what it has to teach the listener or reader.

In the case study below, a Year 6 class have been learning about Viking saga poems and have built up the necessary knowledge and understanding of what features they contain to write their own.

CASE STUDY

YEAR 6 CLASS WRITING A VIKING SAGA POEM WITH KENNINGS

Alistair and his class had read all of the 11 stories in Lari Don's *The Dragon's Hoard: Stories from the Viking Sagas* (2017) as part of their Viking topic. They had enjoyed them all and had particularly liked the parts about dragons, monsters and zombies. Unlike other historical cultures which focused on the brave acts of men, the main characters in Viking sagas were both men and women slaying serpents and battling beasts.

Alistair had told his class that they would be looking at Michael Morpurgo's *Beowulf* (2013). This was originally a poem; Morpurgo had rewritten it as a story. Alistair explained that some people think of the original as a Viking poem and others as an Anglo Saxon poem.

The class listened to the first part of the book where Grendel is described as 'death-dealing', Beowulf's boat is described as 'wind-whipped' and the journey as 'sea-tossed'. Alistair explained these were kennings and that this is a common feature of Viking saga poetry. He further explained that these were two-word metaphors and asked the class what a metaphor was. They had learnt about metaphors the previous term, but developing an understanding of figurative language was an ongoing objective for the whole class. The example he gave was for a sword, which he said could have been a *blood-spiller, head-chopper* or *leg-cutter*.

(Continued)

(Continued)

Alistair then showed an image of an axe. He asked the children to choose a noun. He said that when he gave the sword example he had chosen human body parts. Then he asked the class to choose a verb. He said that he had chosen an action of what would happen to the human body part. The children gave answers for the axe like *skin-peeler*, *arm-ripper* and *gut-grinder*.

Alistair then showed the class four images: a helmet, spear, body armour and shield. He asked them to work in pairs to make up a kenning for each one. He then told the class that they were going to plan a saga poem for a hero. They should choose a woman, man, girl or boy. He gave out sheets with an outline of a human figure on them. The children were asked to design a hero and label with their kennings. After ten minutes, the children shared their kennings with each other.

Alistair told the class that Beowulf meets three main monsters in the saga: a demon, a witch and a dragon. He explained that in Viking mythology there are stories of these three creatures, but also of trolls, giants, sea monsters and more. He asked his class to pick three monsters and to write these on the back of their hero pictures. They were also asked to write kennings for their chosen characters.

The characters and kennings were shared. Witch eyes were *hero-finders*, sea monster tentacles were *boat-grabbers* and troll teeth were *human-devourers*.

Alistair then told his class that this work would be developed into saga poem plans in their next lesson.

In the case study the children had enjoyed a range of Viking saga poetry before they attempted to write their own. When introducing a new form of writing, it is important that children hear or read lots of examples. It is through this immersive enjoyment of the types of texts that we want them to write that we can help them achieve success in their writing for that genre.

FOCUS ON RESEARCH

Ofsted (2007) conducted a survey of poetry in schools. The findings about writing poetry provide a cautionary note:

Across Key Stages 1 to 3, the teaching of poetry is dominated by the needs of writing, in particular the long list of genres that pupils are encouraged to produce. This leads to the current most common practice in teaching poetry: the teacher chooses a particular type of poetry, such as a haiku or ballad, identifies the characteristics of the form and asks pupils to imitate the chosen form. This approach has many strengths, as it ensures that pupils read a range of types of poem and understand the characteristics of particular forms.

The report did, however, caution that the approach was taken too far in some of the schools surveyed:

where it became the only way that pupils were introduced to poetry. It also reduced the number and range of poems that pupils read, since poems were chosen only where the teacher wished pupils to complete a piece of writing. Used in this way, poetry becomes primarily a teaching tool for language development rather than a medium for exploring experience.

Ibid.: 8–9

Show the children the animation 'Jotun – Journey of a Viking' from The Literacy Shed or YouTube – https://www.literacyshed.com/jotun.html

- How can this animation be useful for writing Viking saga poems? What features of it will you use to write descriptions? How will you use the battle scene between hero and giant?
- Who were the two ravens in the animation? How could they feature in a new saga poem?
- What was the significance of the sword? Will a magical weapon feature in a new saga poem?
- Who was the hero and what happened to him? What will happen to the hero in a new saga poem?

Choosing the right type of poem

There are many types of poems, including sonnets, limericks, haikus, acrostic, quatrain, tanka, cinquains and triolets. Choosing what kind of poetry to write in a primary classroom can seem a daunting task. Metaphor is a theme which runs through most types of poetry. This form of figurative language is something which children can find challenging to grasp. Similes tend to be understood quickly, but making the transition from saying that one thing is *like* another to saying that something *is* something else, when it really isn't, can be tricky. If we tell children that the classroom is a treasure chest, a shining light or a blooming flower, it can be a confusing concept to grasp.

The younger children are exposed to metaphor then the more accepting they seem to be of it. Playing metaphor snap can be a useful introduction to the concept. The children could match the correct metaphor beginning to the correct metaphor end. For example, if a teacher could give 'the sun is' then the children can choose from 'a fast cheetah', 'a bright torch' or 'a weed in the garden'. Another example could be that a teacher can give 'the road is' and the children can choose from 'a hairy goat', 'a red apple' or 'a long snake'.

The Year 2 class in the case study below had displayed lots of different kinds of metaphors in their classroom and had been playing games with metaphors before they began to write their own.

CASE STUDY

YEAR 2 CLASS WRITING A METAPHOR POEM ABOUT DRAGONS

Selima had her class gathered on the carpet. She was showing them a toy dragon and asked them to give her adjectives for each body part she pointed to. She pointed to the teeth and was offered suggestions such as *sharp*, *long* and *white*. She pointed to the tail and was given *spiky*, *red* and *dangerous*.

She then showed pictures of different dragons on a PowerPoint presentation. There were dragons from China with beards and moustaches. There was the nine-headed Hydra from Ancient Greece. A bizarre chicken dragon from France was called the Cockatrice. There were legless dragons from Scandinavia called wyrms. There were two-legged wyverns. There were also sea dragons, ice dragons, swamp dragons and many more. Each was differently coloured and designed. Some were breathing fire, others ice, some lightning and others rainbows.

Selima explained that in stories dragons could have lots of different powers, not just being able to breathe things out. She showed the Hydra again and said that if it had one of its heads cut off then this dragon could grow two new heads. The Cockatrice was then shown again and Selima said that if you looked at its eyes then it could turn you to stone. But she also said that not all dragons were bad. She showed Apalala, a river dragon who converted to Buddhism with the help of the Buddha.

She asked the class to think about making up their own dragon. The children worked in talk partners to describe their dragons to each other. Some dragons were good and some were bad, but all had magical abilities. Some could fly while others lived in water or under the ground. There was even a space dragon that lived on the moon.

Selima then told the class that the dragon she had imagined lived on a snowy mountain. It was white and had big wings. She also said that it could breathe out poisonous gas. She then modelled some writing about her dragon. On the board she wrote:

Dragon is death,

Dragon is fear,

Dragon is ice,

Dragon is poison,

Dragon is the mountain.

She explained that she didn't want to use adjectives like they had been using previously, but something called metaphors. Some of the class recognised metaphors from previous discussions and the displays in the classroom. Selima said that her dragon wasn't really death or a mountain, but it was a way of describing just as using adjectives was a way of describing.

She asked her class if they could think of any descriptions like hers for their dragons. She got the answers: *dragon is fire, dragon is scary* and *dragon is powerful.*

Selima said that *dragon is fire* is the only one that would be a metaphor as dragons aren't really fire but they are really scary and powerful. Selima asked the children if they could think of ideas for any other metaphors about dragons. She explained that they shouldn't be what dragons really are. She was then given the answers, *dragon is a rainbow, dragon is the sea* and *dragon is the sun.*

Selima asked the children to work in mixed-ability groups of four. They then had to orally tell each other a metaphor for their own dragons or help each other to come up with one. A photocopied sheet of 'Dragon is _____' was then given out. The more able had more metaphors to write and less able wrote less.

Their writing was then shared on the carpet.

Metaphors can be a difficult form of figurative language for children to comprehend. Greater exposure to it through lessons like the one in the case study above will help them not only to understand metaphor, but also use it effectively in their writing.

After this lesson one child asked the teacher, 'Is "my sister is a nightmare" a metaphor?' The teacher agreed that it was. The child then said, 'No it isn't! She literally is!' The child then went off laughing. He completely understood the concept of literal and figurative language to the extent that this seven-year-old child could confidently joke about it.

ACTIVITY 1

Gather images of any kind of mythical creatures such as dragons, fairies, unicorns, elves or giants and paste these into a PowerPoint presentation. Once the images have been shared, select the type of figurative language you would like the children to use to describe the creatures. They could describe them using similes, hyperbole, personification, oxymoron or alliteration.

(Continued)

(Continued)

- How can this be differentiated for older pupils? What examples can you give? Can the children use more than one type of figurative language in the same description?
- Can these descriptions be improved by adding adjectives, adverbs and verbs? For example, 'Unicorn is as beautiful as a rainbow' could be 'Unicorn is as stunningly beautiful as a majestic, sparkling rainbow.'
- Can this activity be repeated with objects or settings? What changes will you make? How can technology be of use?

Performance poetry

In pre-literate societies, performance poetry was a part of everyday life. The storyteller would sit by the fire and recite lengthy verses, usually accompanied by music. In Ancient Greece, the accompanying instrument was a turtle shell harp. In Africa, it was the djembe drum. In medieval Britain, it was a lute.

But performance poetry doesn't necessarily need music. It has a rhythm of its own. The poems can be long or short and follow any theme. Jim Higo runs open mic performance poetry evenings called 'Away With Words'. He states: '[Performance poetry] has the gift of maintaining its distinctiveness and its soul whilst adapting and adjusting to fit the whims and trends of the transient artistic and musical fads and fashions' (2018).

So it can be about anything at all. This means that we can look at whatever themes or topics that we know will inspire the children we teach. There are lots of examples of performance poetry uploaded by schools on the Perform A Poem website, https://performapoem. lgfl.org.uk/browse.aspx, and on YouTube. These videos can help to show children the many different ways that poems can be performed.

Michael Rosen (2018) said that, 'Poetry is the sound of words in your ears, it's the look of poets in motion and that can be you. Make your poems sing, whisper, shout and float. Let the words make the rhythm and give the viewers a buzz to see you.'

In the case study below a poem is used to inspire the writing and delivering of a new poem.

CASE STUDY

YEAR 3 CLASS WRITING A POEM BASED ON DAVE WARD'S 'THE CAKE THAT MAKES YOU SCREAM!'

William read his class the poem 'The Cake That Makes You Scream!' by Dave Ward. There is a lot of repetition and a clear rhythm throughout the whole poem; after the first couple of stanzas the children began to join in. William then told his class that they were going to write their own version of this poem. The first two stanzas in the original poem are:

Underneath the icing,
Underneath the cream,
Underneath the marzipan
Is the cake that makes you scream.

It's filled with sticky spiders,
Slugs and earwigs too,
And swarms of tiny beetles
Swimming round in glue.

William then rewrote these for a poem about a house that made you scream. He wrote:

Underneath the roof tiles,
Underneath the beam,
Underneath the ceiling
Is the house that makes you scream.

It's filled with sticky spiders,
Slugs and earwigs too,
And swarms of tiny beetles
Swimming round in glue.

He asked the class if they could change the second stanza to fit with his horror house theme. They suggested that sticky spiders could be changed to smelly socks. Instead of slugs and earwigs, there could be snails and woodlice. *Swarms of tiny beetles swimming round in glue* was changed to *groups of ghosts flying round the rooms*. They then rewrote the whole poem as a class.

William then told the class that they were going to write their own poem about a setting that made you scream. They could not choose a house though, as they had already written that poem. He gave the examples of a castle, a graveyard or a cave. He also told the children that they could choose a classroom if they wanted to. Most of the children chose the classroom idea, but others chose a theme park, a supermarket and a swimming pool.

The class wrote their own poems using 'The Cake That Makes You Scream!' as their template to follow. William then explained that they were not just going to read their poems but also perform them. He told the children that they had to perform them clearly and without rushing. They watched some examples of how to perform poems on the Perform A Poem website.

(Continued)

(Continued)

William then asked for volunteers and several children shared their poems. Some children were disappointed that they didn't have a chance to share their poems so William asked those children to stand and find a place in the classroom. The rest of the children who were gathered on the carpet then chose who they wanted to listen to. They went off and listened to the poems read aloud.

The teacher in the case study above did not make all of his class perform their poems. Those who didn't want to simply enjoyed the rest of the class's performances. The poem was then used for further writing opportunities like in the activity below.

ACTIVITY 1

Read 'The Cake That Makes You Scream!' and ask the children what makes them smile. Gather a list on the board. Rewrite the poem as the 'Cake That Makes You Smile'.

- How will this new poem be performed? What resources can be used to support this? Will the children perform alone or in groups?
- What other poems can be used in this way? Which poems feature frequently on the Perform A Poem website? What other ways can performance poetry be recorded and celebrated?

FOCUS ON RESEARCH

Pie Corbett (2008: 1), in his address to the Basic Skills Agency conferences in 2006, began by speaking about why poetry matters:

> Words matter because they create our world and our selves. Without words, thought is a meagre crumb. And it is in poetry that words fall under the mind's microscope. It is poetry that most potently values language, where each word must count.

Corbett (2008: 4) went on to assert:

> A poet may play with words or learn how to look intently at an experience in order to recreate it. They need to generate ideas and then select the most powerful. Writing

poetry involves the meaning and the sound – the music of the words. Sound is part of the physical quality of the writing. The poet listens to the sound as well as the meaning. A good poem takes delight in making music with words.

Conclusion

Writing poetry can develop figurative language descriptions, enhance performance skills and be used to improve creative writing skills. It is one of the most interpretive forms of writing, as it does not always have to follow rules. Certainly, poetry such as sonnets and haikus do have set patterns, but free verse allows children to express themselves in a non-structured way. By giving children the tools to practise their writing shown in this chapter, we are giving them opportunities to go on to write in their own favoured styles.

Performance poetry is also an opportunity for children to show what they have created. We can enhance this performance by using cross-curricular subjects such as drama and music. Whether it is accompanied by a hip hop beat, djembe rhythm or melodic harp, it does not matter. Poetry is about exploring one's own opinions about absolutely anything and expressing them in creative ways. If we can teach children to do that, we are helping them to grow and mature into people that can understand the world around them and communicate how they feel about it. John Lennon (1980) said, 'My role in society, or any artist or poet's role, is to try and express what we all feel. Not to tell people how to feel. Not as a preacher, not as a leader, but as a reflection of us all.'

Poetry can help us all to do exactly this; it helps us communicate how we feel.

Further reading

For guidance and ideas for writing poetry, see:

Bushnell, A., Neaum, S. and Waugh, D. (2015) Writing poetry, in Waugh, D., Neaum, S. and Bushnell, A. (eds), *Beyond Early Writing*. Northwich: Critical.

For lots of ideas for writing poetry, see:

Brownjohn, S. (1988) *Does It Have To Rhyme? Teaching Children to Write Poetry*. London: Hodder and Stoughton (see other books by Sandy Brownjohn too).

Recommended websites

Eminem – Lose Yourself https://www.youtube.com/watch?v=_Yhyp-_hX2s (accessed 3 March 2018).

Akala – Hip Hop or Shakespeare – https://www.youtube.com/watch?v=DSbtkLA3GrY (accessed 3 March 2018).

Akala – Sonnet 18 – https://www.youtube.com/watch?v=_31_UDs7Iac (accessed 3 March 2018).

Hip Hop Shakespeare Company – www.hiphopshakespeare.com/ (accessed 3 March 2018).

Junk animation by Kirk Hendry – https://www.youtube.com/watch?v=17j9FlXvUjI (accessed 3 March 2018).

Jotun – Journey of a Viking animation – https://www.literacyshed.com/jotun.html (accessed 3 March 2018).

'The Cake That Makes You Scream!' by Dave Ward – http://www.windowsproject.net/publish/poets/dwardex.htm (accessed 3 March 2018).

Perform A Poem website – https://performapoem.lgfl.org.uk (accessed 3 March 2018).

References

Akala (2011) *It's a Hip Hop Planet. Guardian* website. https://www.theguardian.com/commentis-free/2011/oct/13/hip-hop-planet (accessed 3 March 2018).

Andreae, G (2015) *Giraffes Can't Dance*. London: Orchard Books.

Boynton, S. (2012) *Moo, Baa, La La La*. London: Little Simon.

Bryant, P.E., MacLean, M., Bradley, L. and Crossland, J. (1990) Rhyme and alliteration, phoneme detection and learning to read. *Developmental Psychology* 26(3): 429–38.

Corbett, P. (2008) *Good Writers*. London: The National Strategies Primary.

Don, L. (2017) *The Dragon's Hoard: Stories from the Viking Sagas*. London: Francis Lincoln Children's Books.

Goswami, U. (1990) A special link between rhyming skill and the use of orthographic analogies by beginning readers. *Journal of Child Psychology and Psychiatry* 31: 301–11.

Higo, J. (2018) *Why Performance Poetry is on Everybody's Lips*. BBC website. http://www.bbc.co.uk/programmes/articles/1FfKxFqx1spNvbHKLNFCXph/why-performance-poetry-is-on-everybodys-lips (accessed 3 March 2018).

Hoffman, H. (2016) *Der Struwwelpeter*. London: Dover Children's Books.

Hughes, J. (2007) Research Monograph # 7. *Poetry: A Powerful Medium for Literacy and Technology Development*. Ontario: Literacy and Numeracy Secretariat.

Lear, E. (2015) *Edward Lear's Book of Nonsense*. London: Usborne.

Lennon, J. (1980) *His Last Interview*. KFRC RKO Radio. https://www.youtube.com/watch?v=1onqhUlBipg (accessed 3 March 2018).

Morpurgo, M. (2013) *Beowulf*. London: Walker Books.

Ofsted (2007) *Poetry in Schools: A survey of practice*, 2006/07. London: Ofsted.

Rosen, M. (2018) *Perform A Poem*. https://performapoem.lgfl.org.uk (accessed 3 March 2018).

Walliams, D. (2016) *The World's Worst Children*. London: Harper Collins.

Whitehead, M. (2007) *Developing Language and Literacy with Young Children*. London: Paul Chapman.

8

WRITING FANFICTION

KEY QUESTIONS

*   How can fanfiction inspire quality writing in the classroom?
*   How can fanfiction be shared with others?
*   What stimulus works best for writing within the fanfiction genre?
*   Can fanfiction be considered independent writing?

Introduction

Fanfiction is an increasingly popular form of writing. It involves using characters, settings and objects that have already been created by other authors and writing new narrative stories about them. For example, you could take a character such as Indiana Jones, Lara Croft or Garfield and write a new story about them. Alternatively, you could use the settings of Hogwarts, Narnia or Gotham City and make them a setting in a new story. Fanfiction is rarely published into books and is generally considered writing purely for entertainment purposes. Websites such as fanfiction.net and wattpad.com contain thousands of examples and have millions of readers.

There are brand new adventures for familiar characters such as Spiderman, Harley Quinn and Scooby Doo. They are often reimagining whole worlds that have already been created. There are prequels, sequels and alternate universes. There are characters who have lost their memories, there are origin stories, crossovers and more.

Fanfiction often rewrites entire storylines too. Harry Potter is selected to join Hufflepuff by the Sorting Hat; Luke Skywalker chooses to join his father on the Dark Side of the Force; and Sleeping Beauty is a boy woken by a boy. Writers of fanfiction can explore whole new possibilities in the worlds that so inspire them. The readers subscribe to the websites that offer fanfiction and create alerts for when new stories or chapters are added for their own favourite characters or genre of fiction. The authors mark their books as 'completed' when they are finished, but often there is no end and narrative rolls on.

Fanfiction is not new. When *The Lone Ranger* was first televised, fans would post new adventures to the production studios. In 1960 a fan based magazine called *Spockanalia* was published. In it was fanfiction based around the *Star Trek* characters. Numerous fans subscribed to the magazine and submitted their own work to it too.

Fanfiction is a form of writing based entirely on fun. It is designed purely to entertain. As such, it makes the perfect genre to introduce into the primary classroom.

Fanfiction – just for girls?

Fanfiction is not often published as books. However, E.L. James was writing fanfiction for the *Twilight* books when she wrote *Fifty Shades of Grey*. She simply changed the names of characters from Bella and Edward to Anna and Christian. The story evolved from there to what it has become today. The books have since sold millions of copies and been turned into a Hollywood trilogy, although they are patently unsuitable for use in schools!

Anna Todd wrote fanfiction based around the boy band *One Direction* when she wrote her *After* series of books. She, again, had changed the names when publishers first approached her about turning the fanfiction into a published book. She was recently described by *Cosmopolitan* magazine as 'the biggest literary phenomenon of her generation'. So, fanfiction does occasionally make it from the web forum into the published world.

At first glance, fanfiction seems dominated by female authors. The fanzine *Spockanalia* featured stories which were written by fans. In 1970, 83 per cent of this fanfiction was written by women, and by 1973 it was up to 90 per cent. Most fanfiction on fanfiction.net and wattpad.com is written by women. However, fanfiction can lead to creative writing opportunities in classroom for both boys and girls, as can be seen in the case study below.

CASE STUDY

YEAR 4 CLASS READING AND WRITING FANFICTION BASED ON *HOW TO TRAIN YOUR DRAGON*

James and his class had spent most of a half term reading the novel *How To Train Your Dragon* by Cressida Cowell (2003). The whole class had enjoyed the book and knew the story well.

James showed the children images of Toothless the Dragon, as illustrated in the book, and how he looked in the movie. In the book Toothless was green with a long snout, but in the movie Toothless was black with a short snout. James asked the class which one they liked best and why.

James then read his class the blurb from the fanfiction *Nraseri and the Viking*, taken from fanfiction.net. The blurb reads:

Toothless, a young Night Fury is given an amulet that has the power to turn him human. Now he must become the guardian of a small Viking boy with a big destiny: to unite the world of Vikings and dragons. But a great evil looms. Can Toothless keep his secret and unite the two worlds before it is too late?

The children were asked to discuss what they thought of this as an idea for a story. The class were very animated about the possibilities for Toothless the Dragon becoming a human. James asked them what they thought he would look like. He showed the pictures of Toothless from the book and movie again. He asked the class to identify the similarities and made a list of these. They suggested wings, horns, ears and claws.

James showed the children a silhouette outline of a human. He drew wings on the human back then added horns and bat like ears to the head and, finally, put claws on the hands. He asked the children if they thought this was what Toothless would look like as a human. Most of the class thought that he would look different. They discussed what he would look like and the ideas varied dramatically. The children were then asked to write descriptions of human Toothless's appearance. A checklist was added to the board for the children to follow. They had to ensure their descriptions included eye shape and colour, nose shape and length, hair colour and style, ear shape and size, skin colour and texture, mouth size and shape, then height.

James supported the less able by giving them word banks of adjectives organised into columns to describe eyes, nose, hair, ears, skin, mouth and height. He supported the middle ability orally. The more able were encouraged to extend their own vocabulary independently.

Once completed, the descriptions were shared with each other on the carpet. James read out some of his favourite sentences. He then asked the class if human Toothless

(Continued)

(Continued)

would have any special dragon abilities, like having retractable teeth, being able to fly or breathe out plasma blasts. This sparked animated conversation between the children.

James then told the class that their next lesson would be exploring their own fanfiction about Toothless the Human and the adventures he may have. The class continued to discuss their ideas as they went out to break.

The case study used an idea from fanfiction and expanded it into a descriptive language activity. The teacher focused on adjectives with three-way differentiation. However, the lesson was really a way to introduce fanfiction to the classroom. The children were excited by the possibilities for what would come next. The lessons that followed were based around this fantasy narrative of a human Toothless. The children explored the idea of other dragons turning into humans too and described what they would look like and how they would behave. They also created narrative storylines for these now human characters such as Monstrous Nightmare, Smothering Smokebreath and Bewilderbeast. The storylines included how human Monstrous Nightmare tried to take over Berk, how human Smothering Smokebreath saved Hiccup and the day human Bewilderbeast became king of Berk.

ACTIVITY 1   MAKING ANIMAL CHARACTERS INTO HUMAN CHARACTERS

Ask children about their favourite animal characters from books, TV shows and movies. Make some suggestions such as Paddington, Dory, Mickey Mouse, Scooby Doo, Garfield, Perry the Platypus, Winnie the Pooh, Bambi, Simba etc. Ask the children what the characters would look like if they were human.

- Could the children describe the process of transformation? Could they describe each stage and what happens to the ears, eyes, hands, feet, etc.?
- What adventures could this human character have? How do they now interact with the other characters?
- Could this fictional character visit a familiar setting such as home or school? What would happen? Can the children plan this as a narrative story?

Ask the children to imagine themselves turning into animals and joining familiar characters from books, TV and movies. Make some suggestions such as *Charlotte's Web*, *Finding Nemo*, *The Muppet Show*, *The Jungle Book*, *101 Dalmatians*, *Ice Age*, *The Sheep*

Pig, The Lion King, Watership Down etc. Ask the children what they would look like if they were an animal.

- What would the children look like as an animal? Have they kept any of their human characteristics such as hair and eye colour?
- Could the children describe the process of transformation? Could they describe each stage and what happens to their ears, eyes, hands, feet, etc.?
- What adventures could they, as an animal character, have? How do they now interact with the other characters in this new world? What would happen? Can the children plan this as a narrative story?

Video games – friend or foe?

Video games have been popular with children and adults alike since the physicist William Higinbotham created a simple tennis game in 1958. This game was later evolved into *Pong* and a whole host of other games in the 1970s. Games like *Minecraft, Super Mario Brothers* and *Fortnite* are regularly discussed between primary school children. With the introduction to online gaming, children can now connect with each other and play collaboratively.

There are, however, games such as *Grand Theft Auto, Call of Duty* and *Assassins Creed* which are not suitable for children, yet many seem to play them, their parents and guardians allowing age-restricted content to be accessible to children. These games are recommended for mature audiences of 18 or over. Other games such as *Five Nights at Freddy's, Overwatch* and *Terraria* are still rated as *12 and over*, but seem to be played by children as young as Key Stage 1. *Plants vs Zombies, Need for Speed* and *Lego* games are safer ground. They tend to be rated as *age 7 plus*.

Whatever your opinion of video games, they can excite and inspire children's imaginations. As such, we can use the more age-suitable titles to inspire writing in the classroom, especially when it comes to fanfiction. The Lego video games, in particular, cover popular movie franchises such as *Harry Potter, The Avengers, Jurassic World, Batman, Ghostbusters* and many more. The Lego *Dimensions* games include all of these worlds blended together. In this world, Iron Man can team up with Gandalf, Wyldstyle with Doctor Who or even Bart Simpson with Marty McFly. The possibilities are endless, as are the writing opportunities. New narrative adventures can be explored by blending worlds together. Characters such as Superman can save the world from J.K. Rowling's Fantastic Beasts. The Goonies can explore a haunted house with Scooby Doo and Shaggy. The Knight Rider car can be driven by Finn the Human from *Adventure Time*. The Powerpuff Girls can save Beetlejuice from the Gremlins. The Wicked Witch of the West could team up with Gollum to try and defeat Aquaman, who has teamed up with the *Mission Impossible* crew. If we can find out what inspires the children we teach then we can use this to our advantage in finding what motivates children to write. Character studies, setting descriptions, dialogue between characters and narrative story writing are all genres of writing that we can explore using these blended, mixed-up new worlds. Non-fiction writing such as explanation texts and non-chronological reports are possible too. In the case study below, the teacher uses the games *Minecraft* (rated 7 plus) and *Need for Speed: Rivals* (rated 7 plus) to write descriptions of racing cars.

CASE STUDY

YEAR 3 CLASS DESIGNING AND DESCRIBING RACING CARS FROM A VIDEO GAME

Jessica showed her class photographs of her at a race track from the weekend as they gathered on the carpet. She explained that her partner had bought her a racing car driving experience as a Christmas present. The images on the whiteboard showed Jessica standing beside, sitting in and then driving supercars, including a Ferrari and a Lamborghini. She described the sensation of speeding along a track and explained that it had both exhilarated and scared her all at once.

She then showed the children an image of her favourite supercar. It was a 2010 Bugatti 16/4 Veyron Super Sport with a top speed of 267.70 miles per hour. She did not get to drive this car, but had always wanted to drive a Bugatti since she was in primary school herself. The Bugatti she showed them was black and orange with a huge spoiler on the back.

Jessica then asked the children if they had ever heard of the video game and movie *Need for Speed*. She explained that she had also played *Need for Speed: Rivals* on her partner's PS4. She asked if any of the children had played this. There were several animated nods and a few blank faces.

Jessica showed them some gameplay footage from YouTube. Several cars were featured, including a Lamborghini Veneno in silver, with a giant green skull on the bonnet; a BMW M3 GTS in orange, with black and red patterns all over; and an Audi r8 V10 in pink, with white race stripes. She explained that these cars had been customised and asked if the children knew what this meant. She explained that the children were going to design their own customised cars with any colour scheme they wanted. They could add extra features to their designs such as spoilers, giant speakers hooked up to a sound system or glowing neon rims. She showed a few examples on the whiteboard.

Templates of various cars were then given out to the children. They chose which car they wanted then added their designs and began to add colour. Jessica then asked the class to come back to the carpet. She asked them to remind her what a verb, adjective and noun were and they gave her the definitions. She told the children that they were now to add verbs, adjectives and nouns to their design, such as *spinning*, *bright wheels* or *speeding, fast car* etc. The children added these and Jessica offered support to the children that asked for it. Most worked independently.

The class then gathered back on the carpet. Jessica asked the children if they had ever heard of the game *Minecraft*. All of the class had, but not all of them played the game. She showed the class a template of her own supercar that she had decorated earlier. The car was coloured blue, with green stripes on the bonnet and white flames over the doors. The wheels were black with silver alloy rims. She had labelled her colours: blue, green, white, black and silver. She told the children that she thought these colour adjectives were boring and she wanted to make them more interesting by adding some labels from the world of *Minecraft* or from the real world.

She asked the children what was blue in *Minecraft* or from outside. The replies she got included *sky*, *sea* and *lapis*. She asked the children what was green in *Minecraft* or from outside. The replies she got were *grass*, *leaf* and *emerald*. She asked the children what was white in *Minecraft* or from outside. The replies included *skeleton*, *cloud* and *quartz*. She asked the children what was black in *Minecraft* or from outside. The replies she got were *coal*, *flint* and *obsidian*. For silver children suggested *sword*, *fish* and *ingot*.

Jessica selected the answers *lapis*, *emerald*, *quartz*, *obsidian* and *ingot*. She added these to her colour labels. Jessica then explained that she liked the stone and metal labels best. She asked the children if they could think of any stone or metal that was red, yellow or purple. The children suggested *ruby*, *amber* and *amethyst*. She asked them how they knew these and the reply was that they were from *Minecraft*.

The children were then asked to label their own colour descriptions using ideas from *Minecraft* or the real world. Soon the children had labels such as *platinum silver*, *mud brown*, *zombie green*, *pig pink*, *lava red*, *crystal white*, *jade green*, *onyx black*, *gold yellow* and *sapphire blue*. Not all of the labels were from *Minecraft*, but most were. Not all of the labels were stone or metal, but they were effective descriptions.

The class then shared their car designs and descriptions with talk partners.

This was a busy lesson with lots of discussion on the carpet and at desks. Some of the children were familiar with *Need for Speed: Rivals*, but most were not. Despite this, the whole class seemed to enjoy the design of the cars. Some went for themes such as turning theirs into a unicorn or a dragon. Some made their car have features such as butterfly wings or rocket boosters. The teacher had not modelled this alternate form of adding features; it was something that happened naturally.

Most of the class were familiar with *Minecraft*, but some were not. Those who were unfamiliar added labels which they could see from the classroom window, such as grass green, sky blue, cloud white and mud brown. The better descriptions generally came from the children who played *Minecraft*.

FOCUS ON RESEARCH

In the USA, Prot et al. (2014) conducted research on the positive and negative effects of playing video games and concluded:

Significant effects of video game play have been demonstrated in a wide range of domains. Some of these effects are desired by parents, such as the effect of prosocial video games on empathy and helping (Greitemeyer & Osswald, 2010). Other video game effects are worrisome to parents, such as the effects of violent video games on aggression (e.g., Anderson & Dill, 2000), although it should be noted that this is a desired effect by the armed services who train soldiers with violent video games. Even a single game can have multiple effects on a person, some of which are harmful and some of which are beneficial (e.g., a violent game which improves visuospatial func-tioning, but which also increases the risk of physical aggression).

Ibid.: 109

Prequels and sequels

Fanfiction not only gives children the opportunity to explore new possibilities with familiar characters, settings and objects, but it also allows children to extend stories. The *Star Wars* franchise has made prequels and sequels around the original three movies. But they have also extended the story by adding new perspectives such as *Rogue One: A Star Wars Story* and *Solo: A Star Wars Story*. The *X-Men* movies and comic books have done the same by adding *X-Men Origins*, a series of movies and comic books which explain how characters came to be.

These are all potential models for fanfiction writing. Prequels and origin stories could be planned and written by children based around their favourite characters. Fans of the *Rainbow Fairies* (Meadows, 2003) series of books could write the story of how the very first fairy came to live in fairy land or how Jack Frost turned bad. *Beast Quest* (Blade, 2015) fans could write about the hero that saved Avantia before Tom was even born. Fans could write the tales of Jake the Dog as a puppy. Or tales could be told of Garfield as a kitten, Mickey Mouse as a pinkie, Spongebob as a larva, Tweetie Pie as a chick or Po as a young panda. *Adventure Time* sequels can take existing narratives and explore what would happen next. *Harry Potter and the Cursed Child* (Rowling et al, 2017) is an example that children can explore. It is set nearly 20 years after the defeat of Voldemort. Harry is a grown man with children. Children could take the 20-year timescale and discuss sequels for their own favourite books and movies. Tracy Beaker could be a mother with a troublesome child of her own. The Wimpy Kid could now be a school teacher with a class of his own. Horrid Henry could be a head teacher of a primary school. The Worst Witch might have a few witches and wizards of her own. Skellig might return to revisit Michael. The Tiger might call again for tea and experience a very different family that live in the house more than 20 years later.

The timescale could be even longer. Grandchildren or great grandchildren and beyond could feature in the worlds of Wonderland, Emerald City or Neverland. It could be 1,000 years in the future of the Faraway Tree, Camp Half Blood or Wonka's Chocolate Factory. These familiar settings might be the same in some ways and very different in others. New characters might be reminiscent of old characters through what they do and say. But they offer possibilities for whole new narratives. Using settings can lead to some effective story planning, as is explored in the case study below.

CASE STUDY

YEAR 2 CLASS PLANNING A STORY BASED ON *THE LITTLE MERMAID* BY HANS CHRISTIAN ANDERSEN

Sita had read her class *The Little Mermaid*. The children were familiar with the story. She had also showed them clips on YouTube of the Disney movie. Most of the class had seen the movie before. They had previously discussed similarities and differences between the book and the film.

Sita told the children that *The Little Mermaid* was first written by Hans Christian Andersen in 1836. She explained that this was written nearly 200 years ago and asked

(Continued)

(Continued)

the children what might be different between the palace of the Sea King then and the palace now. The children gave very few answers. Sita then showed some images she had prepared after searching 'modern underwater cities' on an internet search. There were images of domes illuminated by glowing lights, aquatic railways and spiralling glass tubes with countless rooms extending to the surface of the sea. The children then gave answers inspired by the images that varied from mermaids on computers to mermen in underwater sea cars.

Sita told the class that they were going to make up a story about a school visit to the underwater palace. She asked them to describe what they might see to each other in talk partners. The children drew on whiteboards their ideas of this underwater palace. The whiteboards were collected and photocopied by a teaching assistant.

Sita then told the children that on this imaginary adventure they were going to meet the Sea King's great granddaughter who was now the new Sea Queen. She asked the class what they thought she would look like, what she might be wearing and what she might say when they met her.

The teaching assistant gave out the photocopied and wiped whiteboards and the children were then asked to draw what they thought the Sea Queen would look like. They were asked to include speech bubbles for what she might say to them. These whiteboards were collected and copied too.

Sita explained that they were going to write postcards to their families from the queen's underwater palace. She asked them if they had ever written postcards before. Most of the children had not. Sita then read them postcards she had been sent from her aunt. They outlined the things her aunt had seen, people she had met and what they were like, places she had visited and greetings of 'wish you were here' or 'see you soon'.

Sita then modelled writing a postcard from the sea palace. She took ideas from the children and acted as scribe. The photocopied sheets were given to the children as prompts for ideas and they then wrote their own postcards. Sita worked with the middle-ability group and the teaching assistant split her time between the more able and the less able. The children shared their postcards with each other in their talk partners and Sita read a few sample sentences from each one to the whole class.

The case study is not a sequel to *The Little Mermaid,* but rather a fanfiction-inspired piece of writing based upon the original story but set in modern times. The postcards could be the beginning to a whole series of writing opportunities. While visiting the sea palace, the Sea Witch's great grandson may launch an attack. The children could be the ones who have to work together with the mermen and mermaids to stop the attack. Other narrative storylines during this visit could be a party to welcome them as visitors. The children could describe the food, drinks, dances, music etc. of the party. Or they go to visit the now derelict Sea Witch's home and describe the eerie setting, now deserted and lonely. Or the children could visit the Little Mermaid's undersea garden next to a sunken ship. There, they may have an encounter with a shark, electric eel or stingray. But perhaps the best way to extend this writing into other writing opportunities is to ask the children what they think might happen on their underwater journey.

A SOUVENIR FROM THE SEA

Ask children about previous school trips they have been on. Ask them what they can remember. A usual highlight from a trip is the visit to the gift shop at the end. If the children really did visit an underwater palace, then they may also be allowed to take home a souvenir of their choice. Ask them to describe what their souvenir would be.

- Does the object have magic powers? Does this magic work differently underwater than it does on land? Will the magic last forever?
- If the souvenir was brought into a familiar setting like school or home what might happen?
- What other adventures could they have with their souvenir? Where else could they take it? Why might they need to return it to the palace under the sea?

In the USA, Miller and Pennycuff (2008: 40) examined research on storytelling and literacy learning and reported:

Several studies have been conducted regarding the effectiveness of the use of storytelling as a pedagogical strategy. According to a study conducted by Isbell, In the writing classroom, storytelling is based on the telling of a narrative by the teacher or the student with the intention of eventually recording the story in written form. This pedagogical strategy easily links to a narrative form of writing, but can also help students with other types of writing. In the early grades, story writing is the focus of most instruction, but as students become more proficient writers, they are expected to master other forms such as persuasive and expository writing. Researchers have found that even into middle and high school, students can benefit from using storytelling to enhance narrative writing (Nicolini, 1994; Wallace, 2000; Houston,1997). Further, they discovered that students are able to transfer their skills in narrative writing to other more analytical forms.

Conclusion

Fanfiction is growing in popularity. There are countless examples on the internet. It could be argued that some Hollywood films are already fanfiction. Ian Fleming only wrote 14 books featuring James Bond as a character, yet there have been 39 officially licensed books and several spin-offs including the *Young Bond* series (Higson, 2012) The movies not based upon Fleming's books are a form of fanfiction.

Stan Lee created many of Marvel's super hero characters, but many authors have taken his ideas and evolved them in their own ways including All New Wolverine, Spider Gwen, Thor Girl, Iron Spider and Red Hulk. This could also be considered fanfiction.

Whatever your opinion, fanfiction can be a useful tool for developing your own writing. There are potentially millions of readers who give feedback and rate your work. This means you have a ready-made audience who are happy to critique your writing.

A lot of Young Adult authors say that they began their writing careers by writing fanfiction. Advice from an author tends to be that writing more often leads to better writing. Neil Gaiman's advice is, 'This is how you do it: you sit down at the keyboard and you put one word after another until its done. It's that easy, and that hard' (Trombetta, 2016).

If we can find genres of writing that inspire children to write in the classroom then we might just be inspiring them to write for the rest of their lives. We might just be creating the next authors. If we instil a love of writing now, then we instil a love of writing forever. That is the role we, as teachers, have and the responsibility we carry.

Further reading

For an interesting analysis of the power of story, see:

Miller, S. and Pennycuff, L. (2008) The power of story: using storytelling to improve literacy learning. *Journal of Cross-Disciplinary Perspectives in Education* 1(1): 36–43.

Recommended websites

Fanfiction website – https://www.fanfiction.net (accessed 3 July 2018).
Fanfiction website – https://www.wattpad.com/stories/fanfiction (accessed 3 July 2018)
Spockanalia - http://www.startrek.com/article/spockanalia-the-first-star-trek-fanzine (accessed 3 July 2018).
Nraseri and the Viking (How to Train Your Dragon fanfiction) - https://www.fanfiction.net/s/12455426/1/Nraseri-and-the-Viking (accessed 3 July 2018).
Need for Speed gameplay footage – https://www.youtube.com/watch?v=rgBWCQGY3A4 (accessed 3 July 2018).
Disney's *The Little Mermaid* – https://www.youtube.com/watch?v=SXKlJuO07eM (accessed 3 July 2018).

References

Andersen, H.C. (2018) *The Little Mermaid and Other Fairy Tales.* London: Harper Design.
Blade, A. (2015) *Beast Quest.* London: Orchard Books.
Cowell, C. (2003) *How to Train Your Dragon.* London: Hodder.
Higson, C. (2012) *Silver Fin: Young Bond.* London: Puffin.
James, E.L. (2012) *Fifty Shades of Grey.* London: Arrow.

Meadows, D. (2003) *Rainbow Fairies*. London: Orchard Books.

Miller, S. and Pennycuff, L. (2008) The power of story: using storytelling to improve literacy learning. *Journal of Cross-Disciplinary Perspectives in Education* 1(1): 36–43.

Prot, S., Anderson, C.A., Gentile, D.A., Brown, S.C. and Swing, E.L. (2014) The positive and negative effects of video game play, in Jordan, A.and Romer, D.(eds), *Media and the Well-Being of Children and Adolescents* . New York: Oxford University Press: 109–28. https://public.psych.iastate.edu/caa/abstracts/2010-2014/14PAGBS.pdf (accessed 4 July 2018).

Rowling, J.K., Tiffany, J. and Thorne, J. (2017) *Harry Potter and the Cursed Child – Parts One and Two: The Official Playscript of the Original West End Production*. London: Sphere.

Todd, A. (2014) *After*. London: Gallery Books.

Trombetta, S. (2016) *Writing Advice From Neil Gaiman To Help You Finish Writing Your Own Bestseller*. Available from https://www.bustle.com/articles/178812-writing-advice-from-neil-gaiman-to-help-you-finish-writing-your-own-bestseller (accessed 30 June 2018).

9
FILM AS A MODEL TEXT

TEACHERS' STANDARDS

This chapter will help you with the following Teachers' Standard:

5. **Adapt teaching to respond to the strengths and needs of all pupils**
   - know when and how to differentiate appropriately, using approaches which enable pupils to be taught effectively.

KEY QUESTIONS

- How can film be used to model writing?
- Can film be used in order to inspire children to write?
- How can we embed film as part of effective writing development?
- How can we maintain high-quality writing when using film?

Introduction

According to the TV Licensing Authority (no date), 27.02 million homes or 95 per cent of households in the UK have a television set. This means that almost all children are likely to be well versed in the medium of film and image. The National Curriculum (DfE, 2013), however, makes no mention of film at all, but maintains that, 'Reading and listening to whole books not simply extracts, helps pupils to increase their vocabulary and grammatical knowledge.' It goes on to state that books 'also help them [children] to understand how different types of writing, including narratives, are structured. All these can be drawn on for their writing' (ibid.: 21).

There are correlations between children who excel at reading and their ability in writing. However, this chapter will show that film can also often offer a model for writing, which is important when we consider that many children watch television on a daily basis rather than reading.

Films, like books, tend to stick in our minds. For example, when we remember a childhood favourite movie, this might be a film that may have been watched again and again or we may not have seen it for many years, yet scenes may still be recalled. The names of the characters, the dialogue spoken or the events that happened may still be remembered. Film can be a stimulus to use with children as they can remember these things with enthusiasm. We often see children in the playground re-enacting scenes from their favourite films with vigour. As a child, I spent many playtimes as Michelangelo: a pizza-eating mutant ninja turtle, with my friends, re-enacting the downfall of Shredder and Kraang. It is upon these enthusiastic foundations that we can inspire writing in the classroom. Every film is finely crafted and, with careful analysis, we can take the craft of the screen writer, the director and the actors and inspire writing from it. In this chapter, we will look at how this analysis can help us as teachers to model exciting writing for children to use in order to create their own independent writing.

THE IMPORTANCE OF BOOKS AS A MODEL

When asked the question, 'What can books do that films can't do?' teachers' replies are pretty consistent. Below are example responses from over 1,000 UK primary school teachers, surveyed by The Literacy Shed over the past two years.

- Books make the reader use their imagination more.
- They let you create the images.
- They allow more personal choice.
- They force the reader to be active rather than passive.
- They are more detailed.

(Continued)

(Continued)

- They last longer and give a sense of achievement.
- They are more portable.
- The reader controls the pace.
- They offer opportunities for discussion.
- They allow the reader to see the words spelt on the page, which allows them to learn how to spell.
- They have a set structure that can be easily followed and used as a writing model.

Books can be pedestalised by teachers and, for this reason, film can be neglected. However, many of the points suggested by teachers above can be achieved using film. We will explore the importance of film to inspire writing in the classroom throughout this chapter.

Using film as a model

It is important to remember that when watching a film with children it is quite different from watching a film in the comfort of your own home or cinema. Time needs to be given to reflect upon certain shots or sections of the film. The pace needs to be controlled by the teacher so that the story does not become overwhelming for children, and so that high-quality reflection of each small section can take place.

When we read, we create images in our minds. This can be quite tricky for some children, especially when the content of the narrative is something that they have had no experience of before. For example, in *Danny, The Champion of the World* (2018: 5), Dahl describes Danny's home as:

> The caravan was our house and our home. It was a real old gipsy wagon with big wheels and fine patterns painted all over it in yellow and red and blue. My father said it was at least a hundred and fifty years old. Many gipsy children, he said, had been born in it and had grown up within its wooden walls. With a horse to pull it, the old caravan must have wandered for thousands of miles along the roads and lanes of England. But now its wanderings were over, and because the wooden spokes in the wheels were beginning to rot, my father had propped it up underneath with bricks.

As adults we may, perhaps, create an image of the old wooden caravan about which Danny speaks fondly. Maybe we have experienced them in real life at county fairs, museums or even seen one still in use. However, as caravans of this type become rarer, the number of children with experience of them dwindles. If a child has never seen a caravan like this in real life, in film or as a picture in a book, then it is difficult for them to create an accurate picture of it in their minds, despite Dahl's descriptive techniques. If children's experience of caravans is a modern holiday resort, then the images created in their heads are going to be confusing. If descriptions confuse them or the image that they imagined is inaccurate, children may not want to write about it all. A way of giving children the experiences needed to write about an old gypsy caravan would be to show them a still image from a photograph or, better yet, show a film of how it moves, the sounds it makes, what it looks like inside etc. In this way, film can be used to help develop children's imaginations.

It may perhaps be true that books are often more detailed than films. It may also be true that film structures are sometimes quite limited compared to more complex novels; this can be due to time or other medium constraints, but it is this nature of film which can offer much to the young writer. For example, novels suitable for children aged nine or ten years are often around 25,000 and can be up to 45,000+ words and descriptions within these books can be lengthy. An author describing a character's facial expression when responding to hearing some bad news could take around 250–300 words, whereas a film may show this same emotion in a few seconds.

When we use a text as a model we are demonstrating multiple writing techniques all at once, such as paragraph construction, sentence structure and vocabulary choices. These are all tools that are good examples for a young writer and can be used as a model for when they need to create their own independent writing. But authors often write with carefully crafted descriptions that may well have taken hours to write and which have been drafted a number of times by the professional.

Film can be used as a less intimidating alternative for children. The simplicity of showing a brief clip from a film that shows an emotion being expressed means that any language barrier is removed. There are times when an author will describe a feeling by telling the audience how the character is feeling: *sad, happy, angry, nervous* etc. Ally Sherrick, in *The Buried Crown* (2018: 72), describes her character's anger by saying, *'Jarvis was angrier this time. Much angrier.'*

On other occasions the author will use techniques such as 'Show, don't tell' to show how a character is feeling by describing a character's actions or physical appearance. For example, later in the same text Sherrick describes Kitty's feelings without telling the readers how she is feeling. *'She looked up at him, lips trembling, face white as chalk. "It is just like before, with Papa." Her eyes welled with fresh tears… her voice shrank to a choked sob'* (ibid.: 166). The reader can see that Kitty is bereft due to her actions. It does not need further clarification from the author. It may be that teachers demonstrate this technique using a text model, but when introducing this method to children it may be more effective to show them how a character is feeling in a film, as can be seen in the case study below where a Reception class uses film as an alternative to using a text.

CASE STUDY

RECEPTION CLASS USING FILM AS A STIMULUS TO EARLY WRITING

Alison, a Reception teacher, had been sharing *The Gruffalo* by Julia Donaldson with her class. This then led to lots of cross-curricular work on monsters. The class had made clay

(Continued)

(Continued)

monsters, made monster sounds with various musical instruments, designed monster homes and were fully immersed into the topic.

Alison showed the class the animated short film *Marshmallows* by Stephanie Russell. In it a boy is seen camping alone in woods. A monster emerges from a lake and looms hugely behind him. The boy looks contented at first, but then becomes terrified of the angry looking creature. Alison paused the film at certain points and asked the children how the boy character was feeling. She got answers such as *scared*, *frightened* and *terrified*. She then asked how the monster was feeling. She received answers like *angry*, *nasty* and *bad*. She went on to ask the children how they knew this. The class responded, not with words but by mimicking the same facial expressions as the boy and the monster. Alison encouraged the children to mime the feelings, share the mimes with their peers and then verbally describe each other. The children mimed what had happened on the animation, but also began to tremble, looked all around, had mouths open wide, started to bite finger nails, held their hands to their cheeks and covered their eyes. Alison wrote down all of their actions. The children were then all given worksheets that had a shape to draw a monster face and a shape to draw their own face. Alison modelled her own sheet and the children then began to draw their own.

The class then gathered back onto the carpet and Alison asked the class for words to describe first her own portrait then the monster face. She wrote these words onto her sheet using phonics sounds as she wrote. The class then did this on their own sheets and read their words to each other.

In the case study above the whole animated film was not shared with the class until later. *Marshmallows* is just over two minutes long, but the teacher used it for a whole half term to produce lots of writing, including a three-part narrative story about a monster coming to school and the children taming it with a food of their choice. The lesson in the case study was incorporated into the first part of the story where the children described the emotions that they felt with adjectives and described their expressions and their body language. These narratives were shared with families as part of a talking homework.

ACTIVITY 1   USING SYNONYMS

Read the children *The Evil Unicorn of Doom* by Adam Bushnell (2018). Ask the children why the old woman was hiding in the bin. The text reads, *'She was shaking all over. Her knees knocked, her shoes shook and tears trembled in her eyes'* (ibid.: 15). Ask the children for synonyms or close phrases for 'shaking'. 'Knees knocking' and 'trembling' are included in the text, but encourage answers like *quivering, shuddering, wobbling, fluttering, knees knocking, rocking* or *jittering*.

- What other emotions can be used in the same way? What evidence in the book is there of bravery, foolishness or intelligence?
- How can film be used to complement a synonym lesson? Which films can be used?
- How can this activity be improved with a thesaurus? What word lists can you provide to help less able children?
- How can this activity help with other writing tasks?

Evoking an atmosphere in writing

In children's novels atmosphere is often built up over a number of pages, which can be thousands of words for the children to read. For those children who find reading or decoding text difficult, the act of analysing a text in order to emulate it in their own writing is made even more challenging. The mood or atmosphere may be subtly created by use of key language or characters' actions and utterances, making it even more difficult for the novice reader to understand. Short films can introduce sounds, colours or lighting in order to create the same mood or atmosphere in a much more succinct way. In film, atmosphere is often established through *pathetic fallacy*, where the weather is used to evoke a feeling or set the tone for the desired atmosphere.

An example of this is featured frequently in scary movies. The 'scary' events often happen in the dark, during a thunderstorm, when clouds obscure the moon or when a strange mist settles over the landscape. There are common devices that also feature, such as loud and sudden noises, creepy music or events occurring in slow motion, but all connected with the weather. Children understand how this works because, as discussed earlier in the chapter, they are exposed to such things even at an early age in TV shows such as *Scooby Doo* and movies such as *Monster House*.

Children, perhaps unconsciously, know when they watch *Frozen* (2014) that Elsa is angry when she storms up the mountain singing 'Let it go', because the sky darkens and the storm clouds gather. Disney uses this technique regularly in *The Lion King* (2007 [2011]) when Scar, Simba's 'evil' uncle, is ruling the Pride Lands. The mood is influenced by the weather – darkness, rain and gloomy skies evoke an atmosphere of dark intent and suffering of the plain's inhabitants under the dark regime. The same is technique can also be used to elicit a positive tone. Consider *The Sound of Music* (1965 [2004]): when the Von Trapps are in greatest peril, hiding in the graveyard from their would-be captors, the film is almost monochrome, the sky is black, the gravestones and monuments are white and long shadows cast an eerie gloom over everything. However, as they escape and begin to cross the hills into Switzerland all is happy, the sun is shining, the sky is blue and cloudless and it is almost as if 'the hills are filled with the sound of music'.

In the case study below a Year 5 teacher uses film to inspire writing third-person narrative stories with a tense atmosphere.

CASE STUDY

YEAR 5 CLASS WRITING THIRD-PERSON NARRATIVES THAT INCLUDE ATMOSPHERE

Callum, a Year 5 teacher, asked his class to describe what a feeling looks like or feels like by using bodies and facial expressions. He explained that they would use their answers for developing a description of feelings within a narrative story. He gave the example of being scared or nervous. Callum created the table below on the board using the children's answers.

Scared or nervous

What does it look like?	What does it feel like?
grimacing	butterflies in your stomach
shivering	goosebumps
biting finger nails	you feel hot/cold
knees knocking	heart beats quicker
gasping for breath	shallow breaths
panting	feel sick
hands gripping	hair stands on end
eyes wide open	frozen still

The class then were told that they had to write, in the third person, the opening to a story about a journey to the top of a mountain. One child wrote the following and shared this with the class:

As he stood at the top of the slide his knees began to knock. The boy was biting his finger nails and gasping for breath. He felt sick, like a kaleidoscope of butterflies were swarming in his stomach and he gulped as a bead of sweat trickled down his neck. His heart beat faster and faster.

Once this had been modelled, practised and shared, the children were gathered on the carpet to watch the BBC's Winter Olympics advert from 2014. In it, the narrator is the mountain and describes itself as many things including a 'dreadful menace', 'it summons armies of wind, rain and snow' and 'a conundrum'. Callum explained the meaning of a conundrum and asked the class who was the narrator. The children answered that it was the mountain. Callum asked them if they knew what type of figurative language this was and the class replied that it was personification, as they had been studying this previously. The class watched the advert again and Callum scribed the descriptive phrases. The class could choose three phrases that they could then turn into three sentences to add to their story opening. These were then shared with each other on the carpet.

The children's previous knowledge of personification helped them with their writing. It also was a good way of consolidating a previous skill taught to them. The entire narrative story that the class wrote was broken down into sections like this. The writing in the case study was used as the opening, then the teacher modelled each part step by step, which is something that will be explored further later in this chapter.

ACTIVITY 2   PERSONIFICATION USING THE 2014 WINTER OLYMPICS ADVERT

Write down all of the descriptive phrases narrated in the advert. Change the words by using synonyms – for example, instead of *conundrum* use *puzzle, mystery* or *enigma*. Instead of *dreadful menace* use *horrible terror, terrible predator* or *phantom monster*. Once this bank of phrases has been created, describe a setting that is not a mountain. Perhaps it could be a place such as a desert, jungle or cave. Or perhaps it could be a building such as a pyramid, mansion or castle.

- Which other films can be used in the same way? Are there texts that can support this activity?
- How can this description be used in a narrative story? When will it feature? At the beginning, the middle, the end or somewhere else?

See the end of the chapter for a link to the advert

FOCUS ON RESEARCH

Research conducted in ten primary schools by Gardner (2011) found that linking mind mapping and film was effective in stimulating writing, especially when film was used first:

(Continued)

(Continued)

Greater improvements were made when film was the first strategy than when mind mapping was the first strategy. In considering the reasons for this, we might deduce that film was effective in helping pupils to generate ideas and that the mind map then enabled them to organise those ideas into a coherent structure, which they could then translate into writing. We might make a tentative suggestion that film is effective in generating ideas because it is predominantly a visual medium. Many of our thoughts are pre-verbal and there may be a degree of compatibility between visual representation of story in film and the visual nature of aspects of thinking. It has been suggested that when we write we have to transfer ideas from a pre-verbal state to a linguistic one (Myhill 2009: 48). The use of film may help pupils to visualise narratives and the constituent elements of narrative, such as setting and character, whereas the mind map may act as an interim scaffold, helping the writer to translate pre-verbal thought into language.

Ibid.: 77

Scenes as building blocks

Filmmakers use a range of techniques such as wide lens panoramic views, close-range shots or lingering on various selected scenery, in order to establish the setting of a story. These wide panoramic shots or tight object shots focus on a point or object in the landscape which communicate much about the location to the viewer. The wider shots will show the viewer where the film is set, whether it is a post-apocalyptic landscape, a desert, under the sea, a forest in autumn, the family kitchen or a school corridor. When we view these scenes with children there are opportunities for writing creatively. If we begin by asking questions such as, 'How do you know this isn't set on Earth?' or 'How do you know it is in the desert?' or 'How do you know that it is winter?', the answers to these questions will usually be very simple. A wintry scene may show bare trees, snow on the ground and a snowman smiling his coal-toothed smile in the middle of the garden. Depending on the reading ability of the children, similar text examples may be used to model structure, although a shared writing approach with children's oral input may be preferred, with the teacher acting as scribe for children's ideas.

Just as novels are built of words, sentences, paragraphs and into chapters, films are similarly built up using a defined structure which can then be used as a model for children to create their own narratives. If we look at the way in which novels start and compare them to the way in which movies start, there are similarities. It may be in one of the following ways, which both novelists and scriptwriters both regularly use:

- setting description;
- character description;
- first- or third-person narrator recalling recounting previous events;
- introduction to the conflict;
- a mystery;
- in media res – quite literally in the middle of things.

We explore textual examples of these openings in Chapter 2.

Many films open with an establishing shot in order to allow the audience to know where the story is going to take place. For example, in *The Lion King* the golden sun rises over the horizon bringing light to the plains. As the rhinoceros raises its head from the long grass, the cheetah watches from its vantage point and storks circle over a vast waterfall as a herd of elephants trample through the mist below a snow-capped mountain. If anyone was left in doubt as to where this story is set, then the accompanying tribal music confirms that the story is set in Africa.

This is a similar opening to the short film *The Ocean Maker* (2014) from Martell in which animation begins with a sweeping vista which lasts for around a minute of this six-minute film. It opens with a deserted landscape where shifting sands of a desert are littered with remnants of a thriving ocean; a pleasure cruiser, an aircraft carrier and a submarine are all marooned on the sand, indicating some kind of catastrophic world-event which has left a once vast ocean dry and barren.

The short animation *Pigeon Impossible* (2009), also from Martell Studios, begins with a shot of the Washington Monument. This is a much shorter establishing shot of around two to three seconds; however, it allows the viewer to immediately understand that this story is set in modern-day Washington DC, before quickly moving on to introduce the main protagonist: Walter Beckett, secret agent.

All three of these openings, one short and two long, can be used to demonstrate the technique of establishing the story setting in the opening section. It would be useful in discussion with the children to look at the differences between them. In *Pigeon Impossible* the establishing shot is really short so we could ask: 'How could we create a short opening using words?' Simple examples can be given, such as 'It was a warm Spring day in Washington DC' or 'Washington DC was busy and most people were going about their daily business.'

If we compare this opening to the silent sweeping vistas of the desert in *The Ocean Maker*, then perhaps the opening descriptions could match the opening scenes. Longer, more detailed sentences could be written when examining *The Ocean Maker*. Descriptive techniques are needed to 'paint a picture' for readers and allow them to imagine the vast emptiness and the abandoned vessels. It would be inadequate to just write, 'there are some boats sitting in the desert'. It wouldn't have the same dramatic effect that the original storyteller was trying to achieve. To model the descriptive technique, we need to first look at the language that can be used to describe the desert and the boats. In the case study below, a Year 4 class were learning about how to write structured narratives using the film *DreamGiver* (2011) to show them the desired structure of their stories.

CASE STUDY

YEAR 4 CLASS USING THE ANIMATED SHORT FILM *DREAMGIVER* TO PLAN A NARRATIVE STORY

A Year 4 class had been learning about planning narrative stories. Sarah, their teacher, showed the class the animated film *DreamGiver*. The class knew the story well and, when retelling the events, they broke it down into six definitive sections. These were displayed on the board as follows:

- setting description;
- introduction of main protagonist;
- rising action;
- problem;
- introduction of second setting;
- resolution.

The class then used this same structure to develop their own narratives. Sarah showed them the opening of the animation again. The film opens by focusing on a quiet village scene at night. A strange creature flashes across the sky, leaving the viewer wondering what it was. But it is the setting that is mainly focused on in these opening scenes, rather than the creature. The scene shows a church tower acting like a town guard, with the window shutters closed firmly like sleeping eyelids. It is like a guard has fallen asleep while on duty.

Sarah asked her class to set their story in a town at night. She asked how they would describe the buildings and most answered that they would describe them as being asleep. The children made notes on whiteboards while Sarah pretended to be asleep. They wrote phrases such as *closed eyes*, *open mouth* and *snoring sounds*. They wrote adjectives to describe her sleeping too. These were then written into an opening paragraph for their story.

The class gathered back onto the carpet to watch the next scene. This is where the main character is introduced and we see the DreamGiver as a winged, old, stick-like man with a bald head and round goggles. Sarah explained that their own stories would continue using the same structure as *DreamGiver*. The children were asked to design their own flying creature. These were labelled with adjectives, verbs and adverbs. These were then turned into sentences, with an emphasis on noun expansion and a focus on prepositional language, such as 'from his back, sprouted a pair of fragile wings'.

The remaining sections of 'rising action', 'problem', 'second setting' and 'resolution' were set out on a four-part planning worksheet for use in another lesson. Sarah then asked the class to share their opening two sections with each other on the carpet.

The lesson was followed up with two further lessons. The narrative was planned two sections at a time to produce a six-part story. Once the basic structure was written, the teacher asked the children to redraft their story. She explained that elements could be moved around or additional elements could be added. For example, additional characters could be added or character interaction with dialogue could be inserted. This was all supported with the use of oral storytelling.

ACTIVITY 1

Read extracts from *The BFG* by Roald Dahl (1982 [2016]). Concentrate on the parts where the giant collects the dreams. Ask the children to design their own dream-catcher. They can then design their own dream jars.

- How can the 2016 film be used to support this activity? How can the 1989 animated film also be used? Which scenes will you show?
- What cross-curricular writing opportunities are there when designing dream-catchers and dream jars?

Conclusion

Film can be used in a wide variety of ways to inspire writing, as explored in this chapter. It can help children to understand narrative structures and explore figurative language descriptions. It is a popular device for teaching a variety of writing techniques and offers many opportunities in the classroom. It is important that we use film, but it can never replace books in the primary school. Film is another device that we can use to support learning in conjunction with using books.

Further reading

For further discussion on using film and visual media to stimulate writing, see:

Smith, R (2015) Beyond text: using visual imagery and film to enhance children's writing, in Waugh, D., Neaum, S. and Bushnell, A. (eds), *Beyond Early Writing*. Northwich: Critical: 96–110.

Recommended websites

Pigeon Impossible animation –
https://www.literacyshed.com/pigeon-impossible.html (accessed 28M2018).

Marshmallows animation –
https://www.literacyshed.com/marshmallows.html (accessed 3 June 2018).
2014 Winter Olympics advert –
https://www.literacyshed.com/the-sports-shed.html (accessed 3 June 2018).
Ocean Maker animation –
https://www.literacyshed.com/oceanmaker.html (accessed 17 May 2018).
Dreamgiver animation –
https://www.literacyshed.com/dreamgiver.html (accessed 17 May 2018).

References

Bushnell, A. (2018) *The Evil Unicorn of Doom*. Silsdon.: Caboodle Books

Dahl, R. (2016) *BFG*. London: Puffin.

Dahl, R. (2018) *Danny, the Champion of the World*. London: Puffin.

DfE (2013) *The National Curriculum in England: Key Stages 1 and 2 framework document. English Programme of Study*. Available at: https://assets.publishing.service.gov.uk/government/uploads/system/uploads/attachment_data/file/335186/PRIMARY_national_curriculum_-_English_220714.pdf (accessed 19 May 2018).

Gardner, P. (2011) *An investigation of mind mapping and other pre-writing strategies to overcome reluctance*. Final Report of the Queens Park Lower School – University of Bedfordshire Partnership: Funded by the Bedford Charity (Harpur Trust). http://www.harpurtrust.org.uk/wp-content/uploads/2015/11/The-Reluctant-Writer-in-the-Primary-Classroom.pdf

Myhill, D. (2009) Children's patterns of composition and their reflections on their composing processes. *British Educational Research Journal 35*(1): 47–64.

Sherrick, A. (2018) *The Buried Crown*. London: Chickenhouse.

TV Licensing Authority (no date) http://www.tvlicensing.co.uk/about/foi-licences-facts-and-figures-AB18 (accessed 13 ay 2018).

Film references

Frozen [DVD] [2014] Directed by Buck, C. and Lee, J.USA: Walt Disney Home Entertainment.

The Lion King [DVD] [2011] Directed by Allers, R. and Minkoff, R. USA: Walt Disney Home Entertainment.

The Sound of Music [DVD] [2004] Directed by Wise, R. USA: Fox.

10

WRITING FICTION AND NON-FICTION BY RETELLING

TEACHERS' STANDARDS

This chapter will help you with the following Teachers' Standards:

1. **Set high expectations which inspire, motivate and challenge pupils**
   - establish a safe and stimulating environment for pupils, rooted in mutual respect;
   - set goals that stretch and challenge pupils of all backgrounds, abilities and dispositions.

3. **Demonstrate good subject and curriculum knowledge**
   - have a secure knowledge of the relevant subject(s) and curriculum areas, foster and maintain pupils' interest in the subject, and address misunderstandings;
   - demonstrate a critical understanding of developments in the subject and curriculum areas, and promote the value of scholarship;
   - demonstrate an understanding of and take responsibility for promoting high standards of literacy, articulacy and the correct use of standard English, whatever the teacher's specialist subject.

KEY QUESTIONS

- What forms of retelling lead to effective writing?
- How can retelling strategies develop creative writing techniques?
- What experiences motivate and inspire children to retell using greater depth writing?
- Can oral retelling be used as a device to develop written retelling?

Introduction

Retelling can be vast and varied. Whether children are retelling a narrative story that they have read or retelling something that they have experienced directly, the strategies children use can be similar. Retelling is something that features in all subjects taught in the primary school. In Maths, children can retell how they solved problems and what strategies they used. In Science, they can retell the process of an experiment. In History, they can retell events from the past or the lives of historical figures. By explaining how they have created something in art, music or design and technology, children are developing their retelling strategies. When they describe how someone in their class scored the winning goal in a football match they are doing the same thing.

When children bring in objects for 'show and tell' it is a form of retelling using their object as a prompt. But they are also retelling when they describe their weekend, discuss movies, recall video game achievements, sporting success, remember dreams or even when they tell jokes. In order to tell a joke effectively children need to remember the beginning, the middle and the end. Memory plays an enormous part in retelling no matter what the content is. Yet memory is interpretive. This chapter will examine how our memory affects our own version of events. We will look at events from different points of view and how this changes the perspective of the retelling.

Retelling is usually a device to recall facts from events that have actually taken place, but, in this chapter, we will also look at how we can develop children's imaginations to write fiction based upon their retelling strategies. We will examine what common rules are featured in successful retelling and how these same features can be applied to creative writing.

School trips

Ofsted (2008) states, 'The first-hand experiences of learning outside the classroom can help to make subjects more vivid and interesting for pupils and enhance their understanding. It can also contribute significantly to pupils' personal, social and emotional development.'

When children experience something themselves rather than simply having it described to them then they are more motivated to retell to others. Reading a newspaper article that describes a sports event is not the same as watching it live on television, but equally it is not the same as experiencing it first hand in a sports stadium. When we take children on school trips they are experiencing a multi-sensory approach to learning. The sights, sounds, smells, textures and tastes all contribute to an enriching experience.

When we take children on school trips it is also an opportunity for us to see them in a different environment. It enables us to observe their behaviour in a setting we do not usually see them in. In this way, we are getting to know them better as individuals and as such this can inform us as to what motivates them. This in turn can allow us to plan lessons that capture their imaginations. In other words, we are developing the teacher–pupil relationship because we are getting to know the children in a non-school environment. This can lead to more motivation and participation in the classroom.

In the case study below, a Year 5 class visited Jorvik Viking Centre in York as part of their history topic. The teacher was using the history-based topic as stimulus for their literacy lessons as well.

CASE STUDY

YEAR 5 CLASS VISITING THE JORVIK VIKING CENTRE

Scott, a Year 5 teacher, took his class to Jorvik Viking Centre to launch his history topic of Vikings. On the back of the door in the classroom he had placed post-it notes on which the children had written what they wanted to know about the Vikings. The questions included, 'Did the Vikings drink blood?', 'Did they have horns on their helmets?' and 'What did the Vikings do for fun?'

The museum visit included queuing outside for their allocated slot, but museum staff members dressed in Viking clothes and holding artefacts were there to answer the children's questions while they waited to go inside. The class then went down stairs to a glass-floored room. Beneath their feet was a model of the archaeological dig at Coppergate. There were more museum staff on hand to answer questions. The children then climbed aboard a ride in groups of four. The ride took them around a Viking village. The village was filled with artefacts and objects. The ride took the children inside and outside Viking homes and streets. State of the art animatronics of people and animals showed the busy and bustling city of York 1,000 years ago. A commentary explaining each section ran throughout.

After the ride, the children were then taken to the museum display cabinets. There museum staff allowed them to handle objects and answer more questions. Touch screen displays also gave children the chance to zoom in to artefacts of their choice and listen to the commentary. The visit concluded with a trip to the gift shop.

Scott then gathered his class outside the museum. Using notebooks and pencils the children recorded anything they could remember from the trip. The children made notes and drew pictures. They were then asked what their favourite parts were and, while this was shared, the children continued to make more notes. These were then read to multiple partners.

The one feature that was discussed with the greatest of animation was the smells around the village. Jorvik Viking Centre uses aroma dispensers to release smells such as meat, fish, fire, smoke, incense, leather, wood, rotting meat and even the smell of a cesspit. The children discussed these smells with great excitement. Scott asked them to make a list of what smells they could remember and compare these with their friends.

The class then ate a packed lunch in a nearby park and got the bus back to school. That afternoon the children wrote a description of a busy Viking street, including sights, sounds and smells.

A visit to a museum like the one in the case study above can lead to many creative writing opportunities. Bus hire and entrance fees can prove to be expensive so costs can be difficult for school budgets. However, if a class is visiting a museum, it is worthwhile exploring which workshops the museums offer. At Jorvik Viking Centre there are workshops on battle tactics, clothing, medicine, saga storytelling and more. Most museums offer additional workshops which are taught by experts who can share their knowledge with the children. It is always worthwhile paying slightly more to gain such an enriching experience. These experiences can then add to the quality of the follow-up work in the classroom.

Many museums, including Jorvik Viking Centre, also offer loan boxes of artefacts to handle in the classroom too. These resources can be used to enhance descriptive writing and can also be used as a cheaper alternative to a school trip.

When retelling experiences from a trip or object handling it is important to make the reader feel as if they were there. Adding as much detail as possible helps to do this, but also adding descriptions using all five of your senses is an effective technique as well. When we write using our five senses we are immersing the reader in what we have experienced. In the activity below there are strategies regarding how to use our five senses when retelling.

ACTIVITY 1   FIVE SENSORY DESCRIPTIONS

Take the children to a setting of your choice outside the school. This could be somewhere quiet like a pond or field. Or it could be somewhere busy like a street. Using clipboards and paper, ask the children to record at least five things that they can see. Then ask the children to write at least five things that they can hear. Ask the children what they can feel on their faces, below their feet or on their skin. Ask them to record these things too. Then discuss smells and tastes in the air. These can then be recorded too.

In the classroom, ask the children to combine two senses together in a sentence. For example, 'There was the sound of birds tweeting as wind brushed against my cheeks.' Or 'A taste of exhaust fumes was in my mouth as a silver car drove past.'

- How can this activity be improved? How can it be differentiated for older or more able pupils? How can it be differentiated for younger or less able writers?
- What could the children hold while listening for sounds? How does this improve listening skills?
- What settings would lead to better writing opportunities? Where in your school would five sensory description writing work well?

WRITING AS LEARNING

Copping (2016: 141) considers the importance of 'writing as learning as opposed to writing as evidence of learning'. Through the process of drawing upon different texts and other sources and selecting material we wish to use, we not only learn about the topic being studied, but we also learn key strategies writers deploy to convey information. These might include:

- being concise and precise;
- paraphrasing;
- choosing appropriate synonyms;
- choosing appropriate vocabulary and phrasing for a target audience;
- presentational skills – perhaps changing from one genre to another or using devices such as bullet points or charts.

Memory and retelling

In Neil Gaiman's *The Ocean at the End of the Lane* (2013) one of the characters, Mrs Hempstock, says, 'Different people remember things differently. You'll not get any two people to remember anything the same, whether they were there or not.'

Gaiman then explains that what he meant by this is:

It's the glory and the magic of the way memory works. Memories are being rewritten all the time and the view changes wherever you're standing . . . People take other people's memories, people remember things differently, and if there was an absolute truth at the exact moment it happened all you have to reconstruct it with is a subjective truth.

Ibid.: 173

All forms of retelling are subjective as it depends on the recollection of the person who is doing the retelling. It is important that children do not simply retell something unless they also understand what it is that they are retelling. Memory is essential for retelling, but comprehension is equally important. A Nursery child told a joke that went, 'Why did the pasty cross the road? Because it was meat 'n' potato.'

She retold the joke perfectly well. She remembered it word for word. She used the correct intonation and timing for it, yet she did not understand the joke herself. She retold the words that an adult had told her. She knew that by saying the words in the correct way it would ellicit a laugh as a response, but she had no understanding of the content of the language that she was using.

Children can retell stories and events word perfectly, but that does not mean that they necessarily understand what they are retelling. It is important that we, as teachers, use retelling as a comprehension activity rather than simply allowing children to go through the machinations of retelling.

In the case study below, the teacher not only asks the children to recall stories from memory, but also uses questioning to ensure that the children comprehend the meaning of the stories as well.

CASE STUDY

RECEPTION CLASS RETELLING TRADITIONAL TALES

Sukh had been reading her class traditional tales including *Little Red Riding Hood*, *Goldilocks and the Three Bears* and *Three Little Pigs*. She had put puppets in the reading corner of the characters from these stories. The class had been using them to retell the tales in small groups. There were also character and key events cards printed off and laminated for the children to choose from.

Sukh then read the class *Little Rabbit Foo Foo*. It is a traditional tale and also a song. She used Michael Rosen's version of the tale (2003). It is a story where a rabbit goes through the woods and bops animals on the head. A Good Fairy tells the rabbit that if it does not stop hurting the other animals then she would change it into a goonie. Sukh stopped at each point where the Good Fairy gave the rabbit a chance to change its ways and asked the children to recall what had happened so far. The story follows a rhythmic pattern in its language and repetitive storyline. The children followed the structure well and enjoyed the story enormously.

Afterwards, Sukh told the class that she was going to read the story again but that her throat was hurting. She asked the children if they would fill in the words now and again so that she could rest her throat. She began the story but silently mouthed certain parts, encouraging the children to say the words for her. This became more frequent as the story progressed. The children retold the story with no difficulty due to its repetitive nature.

The class was then grouped into mixed-ability talk partners. Sukh told the children that they were going to retell the story to each other. She asked the children to help each other if they got stuck or to miss out a part if they or their partner could not remember what happened. Sukh explained that she would show the children pictures to help them to remember. She used eight picture prompts in total. These each covered the key events of the story. The children retold the story to each other while Sukh held up the images in chronological order.

The class then had a snack and a break. Most children continued to retell the story during their snack and played Rabbit Foo Foo games over their playtime. After break, the same images that had been used by Sukh had been copied, resized and pre-cut into small squares. Sukh worked with groups to stick the images onto A4 sheets in chronological order. Over the day, the whole class had completed this activity.

This Reception class were given weekend 'talk homework' to share with their families. Sukh explained that their talk homework for this week was to retell the story of *Little Rabbit Foo Foo* at home.

The class continued to work on the story the following week. The teacher asked the children to change the setting from a forest to somewhere else. She gave several options such as the sea, a cave, a house and a desert, but she encouraged the children to think of their own. She then asked the children to change the character of the rabbit to a different animal. The more able children were also asked to change the four animals from the original story that Little Rabbit Foo Foo bops on the head.

The class then told their stories with their new characters and settings in talk partners. As the week progressed, most children changed the Good Fairy character and also changed what happened to the main character. Instead of Little Rabbit Foo Foo being changed into a goonie, their own characters were changed into rocks, slugs and sausages. The final result was a new story based upon a familiarly structured retelling.

In the case study the teacher had found a text that worked perfectly for her class. The story engaged every pupil and led to almost two weeks of lessons based around oral storytelling. Finding a book that excites and inspires children is important. But it is equally important to move on to other texts if children are not enjoying it. Sometimes too long can be spent studying a particular book, which can lead to children becoming disaffected with it. Choosing the correct amount of time to spend looking at a text is something which teachers should do at their own discretion.

ACTIVITY 2   TAG TEAM STORYTELLING

Read the children a story then pair them with similar or mixed ability. Have six to eight images prepared that are key events from the story. Mix the images up and display them in non-chronological order all at once. Ask the children to number themselves one and two. Explain that number one is going to try and retell the story by looking at the images. Remind the children that the images are not in the correct order of the story. Tell the children that if number one cannot remember what happens then they can 'tag' number two and they can take over. If number two cannot remember then they can miss out that section and go to the next part of the story. Once number one has told the story then it is number two's turn.

- Which story will you use? Which images will best retell the story? How can this activity be improved or differentiated?
- In what other ways can 'tag team' techniques be used in the classroom? How will you pair the children? Can this be varied depending on the activity?

FOCUS ON RESEARCH

TOP-LEVEL STRUCTURING

Woolley (2014: 79) describes top-level structuring as 'a method of scaffolding children's writing'. Graphic organisers might be used to help children to 'chunk' information together and to assist them in planning. These graphic organisers might be drawn from computer software, but they could also be created by a teacher working with a class or group to draw upon what children have learnt and to demonstrate how this can be distilled into different presentational forms. As Woolley asserts: 'They allow the teacher to break the topic down into various elements so that the particular features can be discussed and modelled' (ibid.).

Points of view

The retelling of events can vary vastly depending on who is doing the retelling. It is important to consider from whose perspective we are reading when looking at a retelling of events. For example, Hilary Mantel, the author of *Wolf Hall* and *Bring Up the Bodies*, which retell the life story of Thomas Cromwell, combined extensive research and her own imagination to write her books. She states (Quinn, 2017):

> *Facts and alternative facts, truth and verisimilitude, knowledge and information, art and lies: what could be more timely or topical than to discuss where the boundaries lie? Is there a firm divide between myth and history, fiction and fact: or do we move back and forth on a line between, our position indeterminate and always shifting?*

In her books Mantel retells the rise to power of Cromwell in Henry VIII's court. His fall and execution will be told in her forthcoming book *The Mirror and the Light*, which will focus on the last four years of Cromwell's life. Her retelling throughout the two books already published is from Cromwell's perspective, differing from other books on the same subject such as Philippa Gregory's *The Other Boleyn Girl*, which focuses on the same series of events but from the perspective of Anne Boleyn's sister, Mary Boleyn.

An example that we can show children that demonstrates how events can be retold in different ways depending on your point of view can be seen in Zack Snyder's *Man of Steel* and *Batman v Superman*. In these two movies the scenes where Superman battles with General Zod are retold from very different perspectives. In *Man of Steel*, Superman fights Zod through Metropolis, saving the city. In *Batman v Superman* Superman fights Zod through Metropolis, destroying the city. The same scenes shot by the same director are shown from Superman's perspective and from Batman's perspective. In *Man of Steel* Superman flies from building to building attempting to stop Zod from destroying everything. This is portrayed as heroic. But in *Batman v Superman* the same scenes are shown, but also the aftermath of the destruction including falling buildings and people praying for their lives amid the destruction. Snyder uses the exact same footage in both films and the effect is dramatic. As an observer we are given two completely differing perspectives.

These two very different points of view demonstrate how events can be retold depending on your own perspective. In the case study below a teacher explores points of view using Roald Dahl's *Charlie and the Chocolate Factory*.

CASE STUDY

YEAR 2 CLASS WRITING A CHARACTER DESCRIPTION OF WILLY WONKA FROM CHARLIE AND THE CHOCOLATE FACTORY

Emma and her class had shared *Charlie and the Chocolate Factory* as their text in Literacy. They had also used it as a cross-curricular text looking at the history of chocolate, focusing on the conquistadors from Spain and Portugal who first brought it to Europe. This then led to Geography work looking at world maps. They also included five sensory testing of chocolate in Science. The children listened to the sound of chocolate snapping, felt the texture, described the smell, appearance and taste. This was recorded using tables and charts. In Art and Design and Technology, the children designed their own imaginary chocolate factories and described them. Music and PE lessons focused on creating their own dance routines based on the movie scores of the 1971 and the 2005 film adaptations. In PSHE the class had been looking at Fair Trade, focusing on chocolate. They also looked at the story of *Chaga and the Chocolate Factory* by Bob Hartman. This story is about trafficked children forced to work hard labour for the production of chocolate for chocolate factories. It is a story to teach children why buying Fair Trade chocolate is important. Chaga is based upon a real person named Mali who was a slave working on a cocoa farm in the Ivory Coast.

Emma asked her class what they thought of Willy Wonka. The entire class agreed that he was good. Emma asked them why and was given answers like, 'He makes nice sweets', or 'He is kind to Charlie.'

Emma then showed her class a scene from the 1971 movie where Violet Beauregarde chews gum and blows up like a blueberry. She asked the class if Willy Wonka seemed worried about Violet. They answered that he wasn't worried because the Oompa Loompas would fix her.

She then put on a scene from the 2005 movie showing the Oompa Loompas working. The scene showed the Oompa Loompas gathering cocoa beans, cutting grass and

(Continued)

(Continued)

generally maintaining the chocolate factory. The scene goes on to show Loompaland, the place where Wonka found the Oompa Loompas. The clip showed the Oompa Loompas worshiping the cocoa bean and Wonka offering to pay them in cocoa beans to work in his chocolate factory. Emma asked the class if this was fair. Most of the children agreed that it was. But some did not. Emma asked them why and they said that being paid in cocoa beans wasn't real money. You couldn't buy food, clothes or anything with beans. Some of the children then said that it was like *Chaga and the Chocolate Factory*, where children are forced to work for nothing.

Emma then asked the class if the Oompa Loompas were Willy Wonka's slaves. Some children thought that they were and others did not. This then led to a class debate. The children were asked to choose a side of the classroom to stand in. On one side were the children who thought of the Oompa Loompas as slaves and the other side were the children who thought that they were not. On large sheets of paper and using felt tip pens the children wrote ideas to support their opinions. Emma modelled sentences taken from both perspectives.

The children then wrote in their literacy books character descriptions of Willy Wonka. Some children wrote descriptions stating that they liked him, others wrote that they did not and some wrote that they both liked and disliked him. All of their own opinions were supported with examples from the text supporting their points of view.

The teacher only delivered this lesson after the children knew the text very well. The story of *Chaga and the Chocolate Factory* had also broadened their knowledge of chocolate production. It had helped the children to understand that slavery is something that actually happens in the world today. This led to a very mature debate in the classroom based on fictional characters that could be applied to actual chocolate manufacturers such as Cadbury's, Lindt or Hotel Chocolat.

This is a different kind of retelling. It reflects a sound comprehension of the narrative, but also a greater depth understanding of the text.

ACTIVITY 3   CHARACTER DESCRIPTIONS LOOKING AT POINT OF VIEW

Writing any character description is based upon your own opinion of that character. If the children view a particular character as good then this will be reflected in the written descriptions. If the children view a particular character as bad then this will also be reflected.

- What parts of the text show Willy Wonka's character? How does he react when Augustus Gloop falls into the chocolate river or when Veruca Salt falls down the chute? What does this reveal about his character? Does it make him seem good or bad?
- Why do the children behave the way they do in *Charlie and the Chocolate Factory*? What role do the parents play in the children's fate? What message is Dahl trying to give to children in his book?
- Which other characters could character descriptions be written about? How can you help the children see them from other points of view? Which scenes from the 1971 and 2005 movies can you use to support this?

FOCUS ON RESEARCH

THE IMPORTANCE OF AUDIENCE

In all aspects of writing described in this chapter, a key factor in determining the way in which a piece of writing is produced is consideration of why it is being written and who its intended readership will be. As Loane with Muir (2017: 211) maintain: '... *if we are open to the opportunities that present themselves in all learning areas, we will see that if anything dictates the type of writing we are to attempt, it is the purpose and the audience'*.

Conclusion

Every time a story is retold in print or orally it is altered, depending on who is doing the telling. The character of Goldilocks was originally named Silver Hair, and she went into the house of three fisherman. When they returned home they found the burglar sleeping in their bed and threw her out of the window. The structure of the story remains the same today, but the content has evolved from an old woman to a young girl and from fishermen to bears. Her fate at the end seems to vary in texts. This is partly due to selecting appropriate versions for retelling to younger children and partly due to the evolution of stories. The story of *Beauty and the Beast* is a retelling of an Ancient Greek myth of *Cupid and Psyche*. There are different versions of the same story all over the world. The same can be applied to all traditional tales. *Rumplestiltskin* is originally a German story, but there are versions of the tale from England (*Tom Tit Tot*), Scotland (*Whuppity Stoorie*) and Italy (*The Seven Bits of Bacon Rind*).

Christopher Booker (2005) in his book, *The Seven Basic Plots: Why We Tell Stories*, claims that there are only seven stories in the world and all stories are alternate versions of these.

The seven stories are: Overcoming the Monster, Rags to Riches, The Quest, Voyage and Return, Comedy, Tragedy and Rebirth.

Stories change in the retelling as do real-life events. Retelling is open to interpretation. First-hand experiences can assist in retelling but are still very much down to your own perspective and point of view. Despite this, or perhaps because of this, retelling offers great opportunities for writing in the classroom. If children are given the chance to write from their own point of view which they have concluded through research, or experiences first hand, then what they are writing about can mean more to them. If children have formed their own opinions about a place, an event or a character then they can be passionate when they write about it and it is passion for writing that we strive for in the classroom.

Further reading

For discussion and guidance on non-fiction writing, see:

Allott, K. (2015) Non-fiction writing, in Waugh, D., Neaum, S. and Bushnell, A. (eds), *Beyond Early Writing*. Northwich: Critical: 79–95.

Recommended websites

Jorvik Viking Centre – https://www.jorvikvikingcentre.co.uk
Man of Steel Superman vs Zod – https://www.youtube.com/watch?v=WRt_UVxgQZk
Batman v Superman Superman vs Zod – https://www.youtube.com/watch?v=P1UtCevVbi0
Chaga and the Chocolate Factory by Bob Hartman – https://www.tradeaid.org.nz/content/uploads/2017/01/Chaga.pdf
Loompaland from the 2005 movie *Charlie and the Chocolate Factory* – https://www.youtube.com/watch?v=pQ5GgslLgVQ

References

Booker, C. (2005) *The Seven Basic Plots: Why We Tell Stories*. London: Continuum.
Copping, A. (2016) *Being Creative in Primary English*. London: Sage.
Dahl, R. (2016) *Charlie and the Chocolate Factory*. London: Puffin.
Gaiman, N. (2013) *The Ocean At the End of the Lane*. London: Headline.
Mantel, H. (2010) *Wolf Hall*. London: Fourth Estate.
Loane, G., with Muir, S. (2017) *Developing Young Writers in the Classroom*. Oxford: Routledge.
Ofsted (2008) *Learning outside the classroom*. Available at: http://www.ofsted.gov.uk/resources/learning-outside-classroom
Quinn, B. (2017) *Historical fiction and 'alternative facts': Mantel reveals all about retelling our past*. Available at: https://www.theguardian.com/books/2017/may/20/hilary-mantel-swaps-historical-fiction-alternative-facts-radio-4
Rosen, M. (2003) *Little Rabbit Foo Foo*. London: Walker Books.
Woolley, G. (2014) *Developing Literacy in the Primary Classroom*. London: Sage.

11

USING TECHNOLOGY TO ENGAGE RELUCTANT READERS AND AID WRITING

Frankie O'Reilly

TEACHERS' STANDARDS

This chapter will help you with the following Teachers' Standards:

3 Demonstrate good subject and curriculum knowledge

- have a secure knowledge of the relevant subject(s) and curriculum areas, foster and maintain pupils' interest in the subject, and address misunderstandings;
- demonstrate a critical understanding of developments in the subject and curriculum areas, and promote the value of scholarship;
- demonstrate an understanding of and take responsibility for promoting high standards of literacy, articulacy and the correct use of standard English, whatever the teacher's specialist subject.

4. Plan and teach well-structured lessons

- impart knowledge and develop understanding through effective use of lesson time;
- promote a love of learning and children's intellectual curiosity;
- reflect systematically on the effectiveness of lessons and approaches to teaching;
- contribute to the design and provision of an engaging curriculum within the relevant subject area(s).

KEY QUESTIONS

- How can technology be used to inspire creative writing?
- What types of technology motivates and inspires children to write?
- How can we embed technology into effective writing development?
- How can we inspire reluctant readers by using technology?
- How can we promote the study – and enjoyment – of children's classical literature through technology?

Introduction

Technology is a powerful tool with which to engage children across disciplines and, in the modern classroom, can incorporate many devices stretching far beyond the computer or the interactive whiteboard. Digital interaction can not only increase pupil engagement, but also infuse motivation and have a positive impact on the attainment of our lowest-ability readers and writers. Boys, in particular, are outperformed by girls in reading and writing (National Literacy Trust, 2012), but are more engaged with the use of technology for pleasure (BECTA, 2008). This chapter will explore whether technology could facilitate the success of boys' writing, and, indeed, all writing in the primary classroom.

FOCUS ON RESEARCH

Recent research conducted by the National Literacy Trust (2018) discovered that the longer children maintain an enjoyment of reading, the greater the benefits are in the classroom. This may seem obvious, but what happens when a child does not enjoy reading? How do we ignite a love of reading in our most reluctant pupils? For boys, many of whom are engaged with the use of technology for pleasure, the answer may lie in the integration of bridging digital media and literacy in the classroom and this, in turn, has the potential to raise standards in writing. Practical ways in which this could be realised will be explored later in this chapter. The National Literacy Trust's research also concluded that:

- 1 in 8 (13.1 per cent) disadvantaged children in the UK say that they don't have a book of their own;
- almost all families (97 per cent) with a child under the age of five own touch-screens.

From the above statistics, it is clear that a greater percentage of children have access to smart phones, tablets and iPads than have access to physical books. This is, perhaps, a troubling fact, but it reflects the realities of today's society; how can we use this knowledge to our advantage? Could this technological trend be harnessed and utilised within the classroom to promote a love of reading and writing? If so, where do we, as teachers, begin?

The Programme for International Student Assessment Report (PISA, 2015) found that boys in England perform less well in reading than girls by an average of nine months of schooling (DfE, 2016) and thus, as successful reading and writing so often go hand in hand, the reading material offered up to pupils in the classroom (and the writing models provided as good examples) should be given careful consideration. One of the recommendations which arose from the Boys' Reading Commission (National Literacy Trust, 2012) was that every teacher should have an up-to-date knowledge of reading materials that will appeal to disengaged boys; this was due to the fact that their findings showed boys' attitudes towards reading and writing, the amount of time they spend reading and their achievement in literacy are all poorer than those of girls.

So what is making boys more likely to struggle with reading? The Commission has found it is not biological and therefore not inevitable. Not all boys struggle with reading and while the literacy gender gap is seen internationally, there are notable exceptions including Chile and the Netherlands. Something we are doing as a society is making boys more likely to fail at reading.

Ibid.: 5

The British Educational Communications and Technology Agency (BECTA, 2008: 3) published findings on how boys and girls differed in their use of IT. Some of the key findings were:

- The use of IT in education improves the motivation and attainment of both girls and boys, though the increases are more marked for boys than girls.
- Girls use IT more for school work, whereas boys use it more for leisure purposes. A large proportion of this difference can be accounted for by boys' greater use of computer/console games.
- Whereas boys are interested in technology for its own sake, girls see IT as a means of pursuing their interests and furthering their learning. This may help to explain the lower number of females studying IT or following a career in technology, but it can also mean that girls' use of IT is more productive in terms of learning gains.

Consequently, the integration of technology in education can greatly benefit both genders: its use can motivate and raise attainment in pupils, especially boys, and if teachers implement it in a variety of creative ways across disciplines, this may also encourage girls to appreciate a wider spectrum of the applications of technology and go some way to redress the balance of women in technology-based careers.

It is acknowledged that technology can have a motivational effect on both genders, although in different forms and to various degrees. A DfES study on the motivational effect of IT (Passey and Rogers, 2004) found that boys seemed to be achieving more in certain cases, yet girls were not being disadvantaged. The research suggests that IT can help boys to establish a different pattern of working, changing from intermittent 'bursts' to a more persistent manner. To paraphrase, IT can help boys work more like girls.

While, for some, the physical book will never be rivalled, one of the many benefits of e-books (read on a tablet or Kindle) is that they are particularly helpful for children who struggle with their reading skills. Digital reading has been of benefit for readers with dyslexia or other special educational needs, for children from disadvantaged backgrounds and for boys in general, who respond much better to the 'cool factor' of tech gadgets than the lure of traditional books. There are now many apps to aid reading, such as on-screen coloured overlays for dyslexic pupils and apps which will read the text on-screen aloud, highlighting each word as it is read (karaoke-style) so pupils can follow along. There are also apps which provide font and contrast options between the text and the screen for those with visual impairments, as well as a multitude of reading comprehension and phonics practice applications.

Due to the nature of reading and writing and the intrinsic link that exists between them, pupils must first be engaged with and immersed in the language of books if teachers want to mould effective, competent writers; pupils have to read and be read to (Harris et al., 2003). They must be given the opportunity to hear and read good-quality literature and learn to imitate before they can innovate. A key strategy for teachers to make writing less daunting is to encourage pupils to read widely and often, and promote a love of books within the classroom. Teachers of English must ensure all pupils leave school well-read and with an appreciation of a wide range of authors, genres and texts. They should aim to broaden the literature to which pupils are exposed and allow them to enjoy texts which might otherwise be beyond their individual reading level, before expecting pupils to write successfully. As many published authors will assert, writers learn to write successfully through reading books; reading into writing is an osmotic process. As Prose (2012: 2) asserted:

> In the ongoing process of becoming a writer, I read and reread the authors I most loved. I read for pleasure, first, but also more analytically, conscious of style, of diction, of how sentences were formed and information was being conveyed, how the writer was structuring a plot, creating characters, employing detail and dialogue.

Bridging literacy and digital media

How do we 'switch on' reluctant readers and engage them with a range of classical literature to raise attainment in reading and writing?

The Boy with his Head Stuck in a Book (O'Reilly, 2017) was created specifically to meet the learning needs of disadvantaged and disengaged Key Stage 2 boys: it is a short, unintimidating volume, which is packed with colourful illustrations and, most importantly, uses augmented reality (AR) software to bring the characters to life on the page. AR reading is not reading on a device (for example, a Kindle), but uses the device to fully immerse the reader in the narrative of a physical book, adding another dimension to the text. Barry Cunningham, OBE (2016: 7) states: 'Picture books seem to have had a much quieter time lately and are, perhaps, awaiting a revival with some fresh creativity helped by new technologies and new interactions between readers and the page.' With this 'revival' in mind, *The Boy with his Head Stuck in a Book* was developed alongside the Lead Designer at Zappar, an AR company that specialises in bringing to life real-world objects and images with digital content. Through its free Zappar app, users can aim their smart-phone or tablet at an image and watch as the content comes to life on the page.

Most teachers will experience pupils who, at the end of Key Stage 2, are disengaged altogether from reading and writing and favour digital forms of entertainment to reading for pleasure. For a significant proportion of our pupils, their experience of literacy at home is via a screen, and many will claim to prefer watching films or playing on a computer console as opposed to reading. Therefore, some pupils reach the end of primary school without a broad repertoire of books from which to draw upon in the formulation of their writing. As a result, progress can be hindered in spelling, punctuation, grammar and comprehension. This, in turn, has a detrimental impact across disciplines.

The Boy with his Head Stuck in a Book is a digital 'pop-up' book which has been marketed for children age seven to 11 years old, but can be used for shared reading with younger pupils. The text is in the form of a narrative poem which follows a boy who is not interested in reading and prefers watching films (a good character comparison can be drawn between the protagonist and Mike Teavee in Roald Dahl's *Charlie and the Chocolate Factory*). The story is full of intertextuality. The protagonist, a primary school-aged boy with whom the target audience can readily identify, is dragged to a library and literally gets his head stuck in a book. He is then flung into a fantastical world of characters and settings from a range of classic novels and contemporary fiction.

The intent behind referencing a multitude of various renowned books and snapshots of their narrative climaxes was to inspire the reader to read widely and come to the realisation that, like the main character, there are many books which will capture their interest and imagination. For teachers and parents, it also provides a quick and easy hook into all the referenced texts:

- *The Hobbit* – J.R.R. Tolkien
- *Alice's Adventures in Wonderland* – Lewis Carroll
- *Red Riding Hood* – Brothers Grimm
- *The Wind in the Willows* – Kenneth Grahame
- *The Iron Man* – Ted Hughes
- *Peter Pan* – J.M. Barrie
- *Treasure Island* – Robert Louis Stevenson
- *Harry Potter* – J.K. Rowling
- *Sherlock Holmes* – Arthur Conan Doyle
- *A Christmas Carol* – Charles Dickens
- *Oliver Twist* – Charles Dickens
- *Tarzan of the Apes* – Edgar Rice Burroughs
- *King Kong* – Originally by Merian C. Cooper/Edgar Wallace/Delos W. Lovelace (but there's a fantastic version for primary pupils by Anthony Browne)
- *The Jungle Book* – Rudyard Kipling
- *Jurassic Park* – Michael Crichton
- *The Lost World* – Arthur Conan Doyle

- *Journey to the Centre of the Earth* – Jules Verne
- *The Sword in the Stone* – T.H. White.

Because there are so many texts and genres referenced, the book could easily be a starting point for at least a term's worth of English lessons and teachers can be pupil-led in terms of which character, book or author to research and read next. The possibilities for the classroom are numerous: children could write an information text about their favourite dinosaur; investigate what life was like for children in Victorian times; create a character fact-file for a pirate; write spells or create recipes for magic potions; research the habitat of animals in the jungle; or create author biographies. Moreover, as the texts are not referenced explicitly, children can work together to identify the books from which the characters originate and could be asked to find those books in their local library. The National Curriculum encourages teachers to make use of library services to support the teaching of reading and writing (DfE, 2013).

CASE STUDY

AUGMENTED REALITY AND CLASSICAL LITERATURE IN OPERATION USING *THE BOY WITH HIS HEAD STUCK IN A BOOK* WITH UPPER KEY STAGE 2 PUPILS

Adele, a Year 5 teacher, gave her pupils the opportunity to explore the AR aspect of the book; disengaged readers were hooked straight away with the futuristic and technological appeal of AR reading. As with a traditional picture book, children were of course, keen to look at the illustrations. In this case, they also wanted to have a go at 'zapping' the animations before reading the text. Once the children had zapped the illustrations, the teacher asked them to generate predictions and inferences in groups based from the animated content. Children began to unpick the visual clues, some identifying that there were characters within the story that they recognised from other books. One group discussed the mix of famous literary characters and made connections between the book and the film *Shrek* (2001). In the text and in the movie, the children observed some similarities as both combined characters from different stories in a brand new narrative.

Adele then asked the groups to read the poem aloud and they were asked to work together to identify the classic fiction referenced within the text and name the authors responsible. The teacher found that this task gave a clear indication of the pupils' reading history and prior knowledge of well-known stories: children spotted Hagrid, Peter Pan and King Arthur among other fictional characters. Pupils were highly engaged when the teacher revealed the title of each book and the name of the author; they peer-marked another groups' answer sheets, 'pub-quiz' style.

Groups were subsequently provided with the covers of the 16 books referenced within the book and 16 extracts, one from each text. They were asked to match the book cover to the extract. Adele made it clear that it did not matter if pupils matched these correctly, as long as they could justify their reasons for making these links. For example, upon reading the description of a dinosaur from *The Lost World*, one group thought this extract might be from *The Hobbit* as there was a picture of Smaug the dragon on the front cover. Many children, however, did make the correct associations even though they had never read the original books. This task was an effective, higher-order thinking activity for generating peer book talk and encouraging pupils to state their opinion with evidence from the text. The class teacher discussed and modelled the PEE (point, evidence, explain) strategy as an example of how groups could formulate and structure their answers. The opportunity for children, especially low-ability or SEN pupils, to verbally rehearse their answers before writing them down proved useful.

Adele, working with a focus group of SEN pupils, asked them to consider what novel the following extract was from, and asked them to structure their answers using PEE.

> I remember him as if it were yesterday, as he came plodding to the inn door, his sea-chest following behind him in a hand-barrow – a tall, strong, heavy, nut-brown man, his tarry pigtail falling over the shoulder of his soiled blue coat, his hands ragged and scarred, with black, broken nails, and the sabre cut across one cheek, a dirty, livid white. I remember him looking round the cove and whistling to himself as he did so, and then breaking out in that old sea-song that he sang so often afterwards:

> 'Fifteen men on the dead man's chest – Yo-ho-ho, and a bottle of rum!'

One low-ability reader was able to articulate to his peers that the extract must have been taken from *Treasure Island* because, 'the sea is mentioned, everyone knows that pirates drink rum like Jack Sparrow from Pirates of the Caribbean, and his scars are probably from fighting with other pirates'.

Other questions and tasks set by Adele over this sequence of lessons were:

- Which book would you most like to read based on the cover?
- Order the books, based on their covers, from your favourite to least favourite and explain your thinking.
- Which extract is your favourite and why? Which extract was most popular in your group? In the whole class? With girls/boys? (The teacher used these questions as the basis for a cross-curricular maths data-handling exercise.)
- Place the extracts in order from the one you most want to continue to read to the one you'd least like to continue to read. What was it about your favourite extract that made you want to carry on reading it?
- Gather your favourite words/phrases from these extracts and add them to the working wall on post-it notes.

(Continued)

(Continued)

The children, now aware of a range of classic authors and texts, were then challenged by the teacher to find the given list of classic texts in the school library. There was great excitement when the texts were located, many children noticing that one of the authors they were searching for had indeed written other titles and that there were different versions of the same text. This task could also have been undertaken as a school visit to the local library.

During the next lesson, children were given a choice of which book they would like to explore further. The teacher then grouped the pupils based on their chosen text (many of the previously disengaged boys selecting *Treasure Island* or *Sherlock Holmes* to read) and over the forthcoming weeks studied their chosen text as a team-based project. Adele, the teacher found that there was no need for elaborate differentiation; all groups were working on the same learning objectives each lesson albeit applying the objective to a variety of texts.

The children used laptops to create group presentations on their chosen novel and author to present in assembly for World Book Day. Their presentation contained a synopsis they had written for the story; a book-trailer they had filmed and edited; a fact-file about the author; a character study; a setting description; and their favourite quotes from the book, among other work. All the tasks and reading activities culminated with this public presentation, and this occasion organised by the class teacher provided a platform to showcase the variety of writing – both fiction and non-fiction – that the pupils had composed. This opportunity also gave pupils the chance to rehearse, perform and exhibit their work, giving them a clear purpose, audience and context for their learning, as well as a chance to improve their speaking and listening skills.

The boy with his head stuck in a book: English National Curriculum links

There are multiple National Curriculum links that can be covered through the study of *The Boy with his Head Stuck in a Book*. The National Curriculum for Key Stage 2 English states that children should be taught to:

- *read books that are structured in different ways, read for pleasure and maintain positive attitudes to reading* (DfE, 2013: 31–3) – AR reading is an engaging method with which to inspire disengaged pupils to read for pleasure;
- *increase their familiarity with a wide range of books, including fairy stories, myths and legends, traditional stories, modern fiction, fiction from our literary heritage, and books from other cultures and traditions* (ibid.: 33) – The Boy with his Head Stuck in a Book introduces multiple famous texts in an interactive way which children can then go on to explore in more depth;

- *enjoy and understand language, especially vocabulary, to support their reading and writing. Pupils' knowledge of language, gained from stories, plays, poetry, non-fiction and textbooks, will support their increasing fluency as readers, their facility as writers, and their comprehension* (ibid.: 31) – *The Boy with his Head Stuck in a Book* has the capacity to expand pupils' vocabulary. Children can investigate unfamiliar words and be encouraged to use dictionaries, or deduce their meanings based on contextual clues;
- *make comparisons within and across books* (ibid.: 34) – *The Boy with his Head Stuck in a Book* references a multitude of various texts which children can go on to compare and contrast;
- *read and discuss an increasingly wide range of fiction and poetry* (ibid.: 33) and recognise different forms of poetry (ibid.: 26) ... *prepare poems to read aloud and perform* (ibid.: 34) – *The Boy with his Head Stuck in a Book* is a narrative poem and its rhythmic structure makes it an ideal text to perform or read aloud;
- *discuss and evaluate how authors use language, including figurative language, considering the impact on the reader* (ibid.: 34) – *The Boy with his Head Stuck in a Book* facilitates the teaching of figurative language through usage of idioms, analogy, imagery, similes and metaphors;
- *The Boy with his Head Stuck in a Book* can also be used in the explicit teaching of grammar and punctuation: *using commas to clarify meaning or avoid ambiguity in writing; using hyphens to avoid ambiguity; using brackets, dashes or commas to indicate parenthesis; and using semi-colons, colons or dashes to mark boundaries between independent clauses* (ibid.: 38).

Modern hooks into children's classics

The Boy with His Head Stuck in a Book strives to engage reluctant readers with classical literature and modernise these classic tales in order to make them more accessible for today's primary school audience – especially for underachieving readers. But why is the study of classical children's literature still important and how can we continue to use technology to promote these well-regarded traditional novels?

The film industry regularly creates adaptations of traditional tales, for example the animation *Sherlock Gnomes*, which was released in 2018. If children have a background knowledge of classic texts and a familiarity with celebrated characters and renowned plots, they can begin to appreciate adaptations, homage, parody and pastiche prevalent across a range of media, including technology such as films and games as well as literature and the arts in general.

A typical definition of a 'children's classic' is a book which tends to be more than a century old, the product of, perhaps, the 'golden age' of children's literature, covering roughly the late Victorian era to the end of the Edwardian age (Mangan, 2011). However, there is, of course, a strong case to be made for modern classics: visit any primary school across the country and, undoubtedly, you will find evidence of the teaching and learning of stories by authors such as Julia Donaldson, Michael Morpurgo, J.K. Rowling, Jacqueline Wilson and Roald Dahl. The need for the study of high-quality literature in primary school – whatever one's definition or interpretation of a classic may be – is paramount in the acquisition and love of language.

ACTIVITY

What works of modern classic literature are children exposed to in your school? Do they leave primary school with a broad repertoire of books from which to draw upon?

Children who have been exposed to a broad range of authors and high-quality texts can begin to understand factors such as purpose, audience, genre and 'intertextuality'. Take, for example, *The Jolly Postman* by Janet and Allan Ahlberg (1989). The postman delivers cards and letters to various fairy-tale characters. He has a letter of apology for the three bears from Goldilocks, a postcard from Jack for the giant, a solicitor's letter on behalf of Little Red Riding Hood for the wolf who ate grandma and so on. Note how the various letters provide the reader with a range of purpose, audience and differences in style and levels of formality. For children to fully appreciate this text, they must have a prior knowledge of classic fairy-tales.

In recent years, the Department for Education appears to be putting greater emphasis on the teaching and learning of classics. In August 2015, the Department for Education announced its ambition to be the best in Europe for reading by 2020 and, in 2016, *Anna Karenina*, *The Thirty-Nine Steps* and *Twelve Years a Slave* were among 100 titles being offered to secondary schools by Penguin Classics, following a call for action by Nick Gibb, the Schools Minister at that time, to ensure more classic literature was being taught.

Furthermore, Year 6 SATs have featured extracts from *The Jungle Book, Treasure Island, The Lost World, White Fang* and works by Gerald Durrell. If this level of reading is required by pupils at the end of Key Stage 2, teachers must ensure that they build in opportunities for their pupils to access a broad range of exciting and challenging texts across the primary school years. To this end, the teaching of Shakespeare and Dickens to primary school children, who will need to understand complex narratives and archaic language as they progress into secondary school, would be recommended. The use of technology can be highly beneficial in this area. By familiarising children with the stories of classic literature at primary level, we are removing barriers to the appreciation of our literary heritage. There are many versions and adaptations of the classics that teachers can utilise to enable them to pitch these stories at the appropriate level. Not only are there many high-quality book adaptations (such as Andrew Matthews and Tony Ross's *Shakespeare Stories* [2004] and the retellings *Mr William Shakespeare's Plays* [1998] and *Charles Dickens and Friends* [2002] by Marcia Williams), there are also many technological versions which can be utilised in the classroom. The BBC's School Radio website has some easily accessible abridged versions of a range of both older and more contemporary classics to download, as well as animated clips and podcasts which include a range of classic stories from *Macbeth, A Christmas Carol, Treasure Island* and *War Horse*. Film adaptations are also an easy and engaging tool with which to introduce classic tales and there are a plethora of classic novels which have been adapted for the big screen including Roald Dahl's *Fantastic Mr Fox* (2009) and *Charlie and the Chocolate Factory* (2005), as well as Lewis Carroll's *Alice in Wonderland* (2010). Studying film excerpts alongside the text can not only increase engagement, but also enhance children's overall comprehension.

FOCUS ON RESEARCH

Studies conducted by the Education Endowment Foundation (EEF, 2018) consistently found that digital technology is associated with moderate learning gains (on average an additional four months of progress). They state it is unlikely that particular technologies bring about changes in learning directly, but different technology has the potential to enable changes in teaching and learning interactions – for example, to inspire and motivate students. In a research report, the Education Endowment Foundation found that, overall, 'the research evidence over the last forty years about the impact of digital technologies on learning consistently identifies positive benefits', and that 'there is no doubt that technology engages and motivates young people' (Durham University, 2012: 3). However, they go on to state that this benefit is only an advantage for learning if the activity is effectively aligned with what is to be learnt. It is therefore the pedagogy of the application of technology in the classroom which is important: the how rather than the what.

More practical ideas to incorporate technology in reading and writing

- Film and animation are often a valuable starting point from which to stimulate writing ideas. *The Literacy Shed* (https://www.literacyshed.com/home.html) has many short films and animations and related teaching ideas which can be applied to a variety of topics and themes.
- The Book Creator app allows students to write, design and publish their own book. The app allows children to combine text, images, audio and video to create interactive stories, science reports, digital portfolios etc. Book Creator can also be used to help teachers gather evidence of practical work – for example, performance poetry or drama.
- Quick response (QR) codes are used widely – on food packaging, posters, adverts, magazines – and an increasing number of schools are using these to enrich the learning experience of their pupils. They are free to create and the software to read them is also free. They can be read using tablets, phones and laptops and can contain text or link to any online resource.
- *Premier League Reading Stars* is an online literacy intervention designed to be delivered in schools, with the aim to stimulate literacy engagement in children aged nine to 13 years who love football, but lack motivation in reading. Pupils build confidence in

reading, writing and spoken language using online examples from the world of sport to explore journalism, poetry and communication.

- *Fiction Express* is an online platform that connects students with professional authors, encouraging reading for pleasure through fun co-creation of stories. Every half term, three books are published on the website in weekly chapters. What happens next is entirely up to the readers. Using their votes, they are able to decide where the plot goes next. Then the author will bring the most popular choice to life. This kind of digital inter-action, like AR, could really help young people engage with the narrative.

- iMovie, Windows Movie Maker or any video-editing application software often proves enormously popular with disengaged pupils; there are many ways to apply video-editing across the curriculum: pupils could create book-trailers, non-fiction documentaries and persuasive adverts, write scripts to film and edit, or even generate tutorials to consolidate instructional writing.

- *The Fantastic Flying Books of Mr Morris Lessmore* by W.E. Joyce and *The Adventure Suit* by Zappar are other great examples of AR texts which can be utilised in the primary classroom to engage reluctant readers and stimulate creative writing.

- Google Fluency Tutor is similar to a miscue analysis, but makes reading aloud more enjoyable and satisfying for students who need extra support. It's recommended for struggling and reluctant readers, as well as students learning English as a second language. It allows pupils to record their reading and listen back in order to improve fluency.

Conclusion

This chapter has predominantly focused on the importance of engaging children in reading through the use of technology; this is because it is only when children have an appreciation and knowledge of a range of stories, syntax and language that they can begin to write suc-cessfully. Books are our most powerful models with which to inspire exciting, fluent and creative writing, and teachers should use high-quality texts as a stepping-stone for original and proficient written work. Pupils cannot begin to formulate their own ideas effectively in writing without first securing a strong knowledge-base of a range of texts and their key features – that is, language, structure, form and purpose.

High-quality literacy and language is fundamental for children to experience success not only in reading and writing, but also across the curriculum. Successful attainment in literacy will optimise pupil opportunities in terms of further education and future employment.

The 'I CAN' Communication Charity (2016: 9) makes an important link between children with Speech, Language and Communication Needs (SLCN) and social mobility:

> *Good language at age five is the single most important factor in helping children escape poverty. Good language skills are closely linked to children's attainment and the development of good social skills. Good communication is the most important skill for young people in the jobs market.*

Among other features, literacy acquisition is shaped by social, cultural and environmental factors. In today's society, we know that the majority of pupils' experience of literacy at home is via digital platforms; teachers can build on this knowledge, offering rich opportunities to develop reading and writing in conjunction with IT. This may help combat the most frequently cited triggers which turn pupils, particularly boys, off reading: a preference for other forms of leisure activity and not finding reading materials which interest them (National Literacy Trust, 2012). Technology alone will not replace effective teaching, but, when deployed effectively, it can prove a vital tool with which to engage, motivate and raise the attainment of disadvantaged and disinterested pupils.

Further reading

For discussion and guidance on using technology in writing, see:

Bennett, J. (2015) Beyond pen and paper, in: Waugh, D., Neaum, S. and Bushnell, A. (eds), *Beyond Early Writing*. Northwich: Critical: 189–204.

References

Ahlberg, A. and Ahlberg, J. (1989) *The Jolly Postman*. London: Puffin.

BECTA: Leading Next Generation Learning (2008). How do boys and girls differ in their use of IT? Research report. *Becta*. http://dera.ioe.ac.uk/8318/1/gender_ict_briefing.pdf

Cunningham, B. (2016) Publishing advice: spotting talent, in: Owen, A., *Children's Writers' and Artists' Yearbook* (13th edition). London: Bloomsbury.

DfE (2013) *The national curriculum in England: Key stages 1 and 2 framework document*. London: DfE.

DfE (2016) *Achievement of 15-Year-Olds in England: PISA 2015 National Report*. London: DfE.

Durham University (2012) The Impact of Digital Technology on Learning: A Summary for the Education Endowment Foundation. Durham: EEF: 3–6. Available at: https://educationendowmentfoundation. org.uk/public/files/Publications/The_Impact_of_Digital_Technologies_on_Learning_(2012).pdf (accessed 1 June 2018).

EEF (2018) *Digital technology: Toolkit Strand*. Available at: https://educationendowmentfoundation.org. uk/evidence-summaries/teaching-learning-toolkit/digital-technology/ (accessed 1 June 2018).

Harris, P., McKenzie, B., Fitzsimmons, P. and Turbill, J. (2003) *Writing in the Primary School Years*. Melbourne: Thomson Social Science Press: 26–7.

'I CAN' Communication Charity (2016) *Reaching Out Impact Report 2016/17*. London: I CAN: 9. Available at: https://www.ican.org.uk/about-us/ (accessed 2 April 2018).

Mangan, L. (2011) What makes a classic? *Guardian*. Available at: https://www.theguardian.com/ books/2011/oct/20/enduring-love (accessed 1 June 2018).

National Literacy Trust (2012) *Boys' Reading Commission: The report of the All-Party Parliamentary Literacy Group Commission. National Literacy Trust*. Available at: https://literacytrust.org.uk/policy-and-campaigns/all-party-parliamentary-group-literacy/boys-reading-commission/ (accessed 10 April 2018).

National Literacy Trust (2018) *What is Literacy?* Available at: https://literacytrust.org.uk/information/ what-is-literacy/ (accessed 7 April 2018).

O'Reilly, F. (2017) *The Boy with his Head Stuck in a Book*. Newcastle: Tyne Bridge.

Passey, D. and Rogers, C., with Machell, J. and McHugh, G. (2004) *The motivational effect of IT on pupils*. Research report RR523. DfES. Available at: http://downloads01.smarttech.com/media/ research/international_research/uk/lancaster_report.pdf (accessed 3 April 2018).

Prose, F. (2012) *Reading Like a Writer: A Guide for People Who Love Books and for Those That Want to Write Them*. London: Union Books.

Film references

Sherlock Gnomes [DVD] (2018) Directed by Stevenson, J. USA: Paramount Home Entertainment.

Fantastic Mr Fox [DVD] (2009) Directed by Anderson, W. USA: 20th Century Fox Entertainment.

Charlie and the Chocolate Factory [DVD] (2005) Directed by Burton, T. Warner USA: Home Video.

Alice in Wonderland [DVD] (2010) Directed by Burton, T USA: Walt Disney Studios Home Entertainment.

CONCLUSION

Writing this book has been a labour of love for us. We all work in schools regularly and have wide experience of many excellent strategies used by teachers to develop children's writing. We hope you will make use of the many recommendations for further reading and links to useful websites to develop your knowledge and understanding of the writing process.

Much of the material we recommend can be acquired for little or no cost online. The resources and ideas to support the teaching of writing have never been more readily available.

We are committed to promoting the role of the teacher as guide and scaffolder of children's writing and we share Vygotsky's view that 'What the child can do in cooperation today, he can do alone tomorrow' (Vygotsky, 1986: 188), which is encapsulated in his *zone of proximal development*.

We recognise that some teachers lack confidence in their own writing and may be reluctant to act as role models for their pupils, but our experience suggests that with guidance and support all primary teachers can play an important role in modelling exciting writing.

Adam Bushnell

Rob Smith

David Waugh

November 2018

Reference

Vygotsky, L.S. (1986) *Thought and Language* (trans., rev. and ed. A. Kozulin). Cambridge, MA: MIT Press.

INDEX